10

MINUTE GUIDE TO

BUSINESS RESEARCH ON THE NET

by Thomas Pack

A Division of Macmillan Computer Publishing
201 West 103rd Street, Indianapolis, Indiana 46290 USA

©1997 by Que® Corporation

International Standard Book Number: 0-7897-1170-2

Library of Congress Catalog Card Number: 97-65008

99 98 97   8 7 6 5 4 3 2 1

Interpretation of the printing code: the rightmost number of the first series of numbers is the year of the book's printing; the rightmost number of the second series of numbers is the number of the book's printing. For example, a printing code of 97-1 shows that the first printing of the book occurred in 1997.

Printed in the United States of America

Publisher Roland Elgey

Editorial Services Director Elizabeth Keaffaber

Publishing Director Lynn E. Zingraf

Acquistions Editor Martha O'Sullivan

Acquistions Coordinator Michelle R. Newcomb

Managing Editor Michael Cunningham

Product Development Specialist Henly Wolin

Production Editor Mark Enochs

Cover Designer Dan Armstrong

Book Designer Glenn Larsen

Technical Specialist Nadeem Muhammed

Indexers Tim Taylor, Becky Hornyak

Production Angela Calvert, Mary Hunt, Malinda Kuhn, Maureen West

Special thanks to Mark Totleben, Nadeem Muhammed, and Christy Gleeson for ensuring the technical accuracy of this book.

CONTENTS

FOREWORD

Searching the Internet has become a hot topic, but business information has been available online for more than two decades. The difference between then and now is one of accessibility. In the past, professional researchers often needed to use arcane search languages to find and retrieve information from complex systems. Today, information tools such as Web browsers are widely available, and they make it easy to access high-quality online business resources.

In the *Ten Minute Guide to Business Research on the Net*, Thomas Pack explains the best methods for finding and using those resources. When he and I worked for the electronic publishing company UMI, he helped me develop several speeches and presentations, so I know he has the ability not only to communicate ideas but also to take a broad, complex topic and break it down into understandable parts.

He demonstrates that skill in this book. It will be especially useful for managers, executives, business students, instructors, investors, job seekers, and anyone else who needs a quick, practical introduction to business research on the Net.

Joe Fitzsimmons
Retired President, CEO, and Chairman, UMI (a Bell & Howell company)

Introduction

How Do Businesses Use Information on the Net?

At the international pharmaceutical company SmithKline Beecham, an analyst monitors the company's competitors simply by visiting their Web pages.

At the news release service PR Newswire, a vice president searches Internet newsgroups to prepare for meetings with clients.

At the management consulting firm McKinsey & Company, which has offices in 35 countries, more than 450 "knowledge workers" gather information from online databases. The firm's consultants use the information to develop solutions for their clients' problems.

"McKinsey is an information-intensive organization," says Roger Ferguson, the company's Director of Research and Information, "and our employees work in a knowledge-driven profession."

Information-intensive and knowledge-driven are terms that describe much of today's business environment. Success often depends on being able to find the data you need when you need it.

The Internet is a system that can provide a great deal of that information. The Net combines some of the best features of other media, including books, magazines, newspapers, movies, television, and even radio. At the same time, the Internet is an entirely new medium that facilities the ability to find specific details in vast information collections.

More people are discovering the Internet every day. According to the online research firm Jupiter Communications, 36 million households will be connected to the Internet by the year 2000. That's up from 9.6 million in 1995.

For businesses, the Internet provides a new way to communicate with customers, a new way to complete transactions, and a new way to become "knowledge-driven." Small companies are using the Net to compete with much larger firms. Large firms are using it to find out how to improve many different departments and business functions. Companies of all types and sizes are turning to the Net to enhance their operations and prosper in today's global marketplace.

How This Ten Minute Guide Will Help

This book is a step-by-step introduction to the variety of business information available online. You'll find everything you need to know in order to access, retrieve, and use information from the top business resources.

Each lesson is designed to give you the research skills you need in ten minutes or fewer. You can jump around in the book and explore only those lessons focusing on the specific types of information that will help you do your job. Or you may want to go through the book lesson-by-lesson to master the basics of many different types of business research. However you approach this material, you'll find that you have acquired skills that can help you not only with special research projects but also with day-to-day business tasks.

How to Use the 10 Minute Guide to Business Research on the Net

If you are new to online searching, start with Lesson 1. It explains the Internet, the Web, and helps you choose an Internet service provider. Even if you are an experienced searcher you may want to read the overview of business information available online.

To help you move quickly and easily through the lessons, this book uses a number of standard conventions. They will help you spot especially important details. For example:

- Text displayed on your computer screen will be printed in **bold** type.

- Buttons, icons, menu items, and text you click will appear in color type.

- Text you type will be printed in **bold color** type.

You also will find important notes set off from the main text in boxes such as these:

Plain English   These boxes explain new or technical terms.

Timesaver Tips   These boxes highlight shortcuts or other quick ways to get a job done.

Panic Button   These boxes warn you of common problems and offer solutions.

A NOTE ABOUT TRADEMARKS

Trademarks, service marks, and other corporate property mentioned in this book are indicated by appropriate capitalization (for example, Microsoft Internet Explorer, Netscape Navigator, America Online).

Every effort has been made to ensure the accuracy of this information. If there is any inappropriate capitalization, it has no effect on the ownership or validity of a trademark or service mark. Also please note that all Web pages shown in this book are the property of their publishers.

UNDERSTANDING THE INTERNET

In this lesson you will learn the basics of the Internet and the World Wide Web, find out how to choose an Internet service provider, and find out about the types of business information available online.

WHAT IS THE INTERNET? WHAT IS THE WORLD WIDE WEB?

The Internet is simply a network of computer networks. It links tens of millions of computers in homes, companies, educational institutions, and government agencies worldwide. Many of these organizations make large collections of information available through the Internet.

You can become part of the network through your own computer. When you do, you can tap into many of the information collections created by others.

The World Wide Web (also called the Web or WWW) is the multimedia part of the Internet. Organizations and individuals publish "pages" on the Web. Pages can contain any combination of text, photos, maps, diagrams, audio, video, and links to other pages. Web publishers organize collections of pages and make them available through a single site.

 Web Page A single document on the Web. It can contain text, images, audio, and links to other pages.

Besides the Web, there are many other facets to the Net, including gopher sites, ftp, newsgroups, and Internet Relay Chat. These are areas you may want to explore as you begin to understand the

Internet, but this book primarily focuses on Web sites. They often offer the best and the easiest-to-use business information. You *will* find details on business newsgroups in Lesson 14, "Using Newsgroups to Gather Information."

> **Web Site** A collection of Web pages developed and maintained by an organization or an individual.

What do you need to access the Internet? Basically, you need a computer, a fast modem, a phone line, Internet software, and an account with an online service or an Internet Service Provider. Many machines on the market now—everything from televisions to hand-held devices—promise Internet access, but to use online business information effectively, you usually need a powerful computer that will let you store and process the information you find.

Modem speed is measured in bits per second (bps). To use the Web, you need at least a 14,400 bps modem. But that is a bare minimum. Moving around the Web at that speed can be very slow going, especially when you're accessing Web pages with a lot of images. As a rule of thumb, get the fastest modem you can afford.

If you plan to spend a lot of time online and you have only one phone line, you may want to consider installing another. Otherwise, outside calls won't get through when you're connected to the Net. You also may want to consider installing an ISDN (Integrated Services Digital Network) line. ISDN is a set of telecommunications standards that can send and receive data over phone lines at up to 128,000 bps. The downside is that your phone company will charge you premium prices to install and operate an ISDN line. You also will need a special ISDN modem. And besides, regular modems are getting faster all the time.

Of course, you don't need to worry about any of this if you are lucky enough to work for an organization that already provides a high-speed Internet connection.

BROWSING THE WEB

You can get the software you need to connect to the Internet from your service provider (described in the next section). An important part of the software is called a browser. It lets you access the millions of sites on the Web. The most popular browsers are Netscape Navigator and Microsoft Internet Explorer (see Figure 1.1). Both are powerful browsers with similar features and functions, including the ability to connect with Web pages, move back and forth between them, download and save information, and make secure transactions (for example, transactions that provide protection for personal information such as credit card numbers).

FIGURE 1.1   Microsoft's Internet Explorer is a popular and powerful Web browser.

Online services such as America Online, CompuServe, and The Microsoft Network include a browser as part of the software they give you to connect to their services. Many online services also let

you use one of the more popular browsers. Figure 1.2 shows
America Online's version of Netscape Navigator.

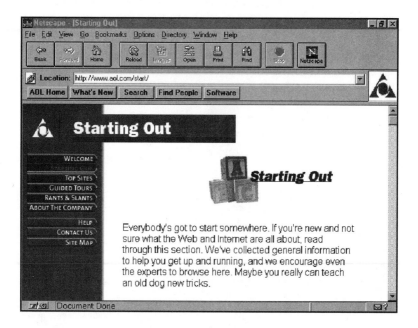

FIGURE 1.2   America Online offers subscribers a customized
version of Netscape Navigator.

To access a Web page, you connect to the Internet through your
browser. The first page you see is called a home page. It usually is
a page maintained by your Internet provider. Many providers let
you customize this page so you're presented with the type of information that interests you every time you connect.

You can go to other sites on the Web by entering an address in
your browser's address window, located at the top of the large
window in which you view Web pages. A Web site address is
called an URL, which stands for Uniform Resource Locator. The
acronym is pronounced "Earl." It tells your browser where to find
the site you're looking for. URLs start with the letters http, which
stands for HyperText Transfer Protocol (for example, the URL for
The New York Times is **http://www.nytimes.com**).

You also can go to other sites and pages on the Web simply by pointing with your cursor and clicking with your mouse. The items you click include buttons, icons, and highlighted text. These items represent links to other pages, either within the Web site you're visiting or to a completely different site. You can tell when your cursor is pointing at a link because it turns from an arrow into a pointing finger.

CHOOSING AN INTERNET PROVIDER

To get started on the Web, you need to establish an account with an online service or an Internet Service Provider (also known as an ISP). Online services include America Online (1-800-827-6364), CompuServe (1-800-848-8990), Prodigy (1-800-213-0992), and The Microsoft Network (1-800-386-5550).

All these services provide Internet access as well as their own well organized collections of online information (including a great deal of business information). The services offer several different pricing plans, including "fee-plus" accounts, which charge a set fee for a few hours of usage per month (usually about $10 for five hours). You'll pay between $2.00 and $2.50 for each additional hour.

Some ISPs operate on a national level and sign up members from all over the country. These include SpryNet (1-206-957-8998), IBM Internet Connection Service (1-800-821-4612), Concentric Network (1-800-745-2747), IDT Internet Services (1-201-883-2000), and Whole Earth Networks (1-415-281-6500).

Other ISPs operate on a local level. Look for them under Internet Service Providers in your Yellow Pages. If you travel a lot, a national provider may be your best choice so you can get connected when you're on the road.

Many telephone companies have entered the ISP business, too— for example, AT&T Worldnet Service (1-800-400-1447) and MCI Internet (1-800-550-0930).

In the past, online services have been easier to set up and use than ISPs, but online services usually were more expensive because of their high per-hour charges. ISPs also tended to offer more powerful Web browsers and other Internet access tools, including e-mail, newsgroup, and chat applications.

Today, the differences between online services and ISPs are becoming less discernible. Many online services are offering flat-rate pricing plans that provide unlimited access for a fixed fee of $19.95 per month, which is the same rate most ISPs charge. (A flat-fee plan is your best value if you spend more than fifteen hours online per month.) In addition, most online services now provide powerful Internet access tools, including the Web browser of your choice.

Many online services and ISPs offer free trial periods you can use to explore their services without incurring online charges. Take advantage of this time to evaluate a service before you make a commitment. Here are some evaluation tips:

- Make sure the provider lets you access the Internet through a local dial-up number or a toll-free 800 number. You don't want to pay long-distance charges in addition to the online fee.

- Make sure the provider has adequate technical support and customer service. If you have to wait an extremely long time on a support line, you should choose another provider.

- Make sure the provider's technicians can explain answers to your questions in terms you can understand. If you need assistance installing your software or learning how to use it, the technicians should be ready, willing, and able to help.

- Make sure the provider has sufficient bandwidth, which means they should have the technological ability to handle a lot of Internet traffic without busy signals, slowdowns, or access problems. You should be warned, however, that some slowdowns on the Web are inevitable, especially during peak hours, which usually are the early evening hours when most people use the system at home. Still, some providers exacerbate the problem because they have overextended phone lines and modems. If you consistently encounter slowdowns or access problems, the problems may lie with the service provider.

To help you compare providers, you can access a Web site called The Ultimate Guide to Internet Service Providers (see Figure 1.3). It offers reviews of ISPs and ranks them according to ratings submitted by Internet users who have registered to become members of CNET, the site that sponsors the Ultimate Guide. You don't need to be a member to read the reviews.

FIGURE 1.3 The Ultimate Guide to Internet Service Providers offers reviews and ratings of ISPs.

Of course, you do need Internet access before you can search the site. If you don't have it yet, perhaps you can perform this lesson on the computer of a friend or colleague who does. If you already have an Internet provider, this lesson may show how other services compare to yours.

To find information at the Ultimate Guide to Internet Service Providers:

1. Type the URL **http://www.cnet.com/Content/Reviews/ Compare/ISP/** into your Web browser's address box and press Enter.

2. When the welcome screen appears, scroll down and click on the text that says Top National ISPs.

3. Scroll down to the list of ISPs. Reviews are available for the ones that have stars next to their names.

4. To read a review, click on the ISP's name. If you click a name without a star, your Web browser will take you to that provider's site. After you read a review or visit a site, you can use the Back button on your browser to return to the list of top ISPs.

5. If you want to find information on ISPs in your area, click the All ISPs button beneath the list of top ISPs.

6. Scroll down the All ISPs page and click the Search by area(s) served button (see Figure 1.4).

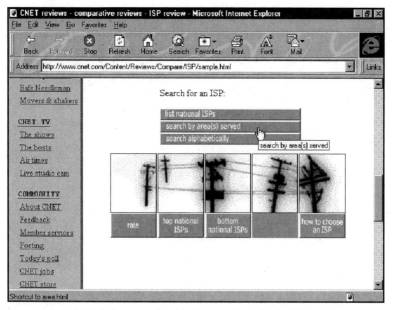

FIGURE 1.4   Click here to find information about ISPs in your state.

7. Select your state from the list in the box and click the Submit button.

8. Like the list of top ISPs, the list of providers in your state offers reviews for the services that have stars next to their names. If you click on the name of an ISP without a star, the link will take you to the ISP's site.

Other Web sites that may help you find ISPs include:

- The Web directory **Yahoo!** offers links to U.S., regional, and international ISPs. The site also provides a directory of other ISP directories. To use Yahoo!, go to the URL **http://www.yahoo.com,** and then select the following categories and subcategories: **Business and Economy, Companies, Internet Services, Internet Access Providers.**

- **The List (http://www.thelist.com)** also provides information on ISPs around the world. For U.S. or Canadian ISPs, you can search by state or province.

USING THE INTERNET CONNECTION WIZARD

Microsoft's Internet Connection Wizard offers an especially easy way to get on the Internet. It provides access to worldwide ISPs through a centralized service, and it offers detailed instructions throughout the sign-up process.

The wizard is included with later releases of Windows 95 and Internet Explorer as well as the Microsoft Plus! Windows add-on program. To see if you have the wizard on your computer, search for the file Inetwiz.exe. You may be able to run it by clicking the Start button and then selecting Programs, Accessories, Internet Tools, and Get on the Internet.

If you don't have the program, you can download the latest version of Microsoft Internet Explorer from **http://www.microsoft.com/ie/download/.**

When you run the Internet Connection Wizard, it will walk you through the process of getting on the Net step-by-step. You can use the program to set up a connection through a regular phone line or a local area network.

WHAT TYPE OF BUSINESS INFORMATION IS AVAILABLE ONLINE?

Now you have access to the Internet and you're ready to search the Web. What type of business information can you find?

Company profiles, trade data, business news, corporate tax and legal advice, small business information, prepared forms and documents, biographies of executives, financial reports— and that's just the beginning. It's all out there in cyberspace. Much of it is free. Some of it costs a low fee. Some of it is very expensive. Whenever possible, this book focuses on how to find no- or low-cost information from high-quality Internet resources. But sometimes you may find that paying for more expensive data is worth it if it helps your business or your career.

Identifying high-quality, reliable resources can be challenging because, as some online observers have noted, three months equals one year on the Internet. In other words, the online world changes very rapidly. Web sites remodel their interfaces. New companies, services, products, and technologies seem to emerge daily. Others disappear without warning. Information you find on the Web one day may not be there the next. Prices are especially susceptible to change because companies that do business on the Net are still trying to develop the best business models.

Whenever possible, this book focuses on Internet information created by established companies, government institutions, and other types of organizations. But there are no guarantees, and the inclusion of any Web site in this book doesn't necessarily constitute an endorsement of its products or services.

Still, several different types of Web sites can be especially useful for businesspeople:

- Corporate sites—Many companies have created sites with information on their products or services as well as a company history or profile.

- Databases—Many sites include large collections of information and interfaces that help you pinpoint the information you need.

- Directories—Some sites are guides to other sites.

- Electronic publications—The Web provides electronic versions of traditional newspapers and magazines as well as digital publications that exist only online.

- News services—These can provide details on breaking business news stories.

- Transactional sites—These sites let you perform a transaction online. For example, some sites let you make online travel reservations.

Whatever type of site you use, you will discover that the Internet is a powerful tool that can help you with both day-to-day business activities and far-reaching corporate strategies.

In this lesson you learned basic details about the Internet, the Web, and the types of business information available online. In the next lesson, you will learn how to use Web search engines.

L_ESS_ON 2

SEARCHING THE WEB

In this lesson, you'll learn how to use Web search engines to find the information you need.

WHAT ARE SEARCH ENGINES?

When you browse the Web, you jump from one site to another. You follow links that provide additional information on your topic. When you search the Web, you're looking for a specific site or a specific type of information. How can you find it among the millions of Web pages?

You use search engine sites. They are based on a technology that continually crawls around the Internet, indexes millions of pages, and stores the information in a massive database. Search engine sites let you enter keywords on their pages and then generate a list of "hits" that provide links to the Web pages or other types of Internet information containing your keywords. Search engine sites usually are supported by online advertising so their services are free to any Web user.

Keywords   Words or phrases describing the information you want to find. Keywords can be the names of people, companies, or Web sites. They also can be subject terms such as "international trade" or "printing companies."

Hits   Items in your search results list that were retrieved by your keywords. When you're using search engines, hits usually are links to other sites. If you were searching a database of documents—newspaper articles, for example— hits would refer to the articles your keywords retrieved.

A Sample Search with Excite

Excite is a search engine that indexes more than 50 million Web pages. To begin an Excite search:

1. Type the URL **http://www.excite.com** in your Web browser's address box and press Enter.

2. When Excite's Web page appears on your screen, enter your keywords in the search entry box and click the Search button next to it. In Figure 2.1, the user has entered the keywords **marketing organizations**.

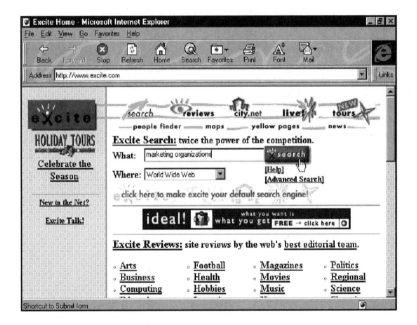

FIGURE 2.1   Excite can help you find information in more than 50 million Web pages.

3. When the results page appears, scroll through the list. You will see links to many different types of Web pages. The percentage sign to the left of each result is a confidence rating. The closer the rating is to 100 percent, the

more confident the search engine is that the document *i.e. web page!* will fit your needs. As you browse through the list, you will see that some of the sites are relevant to the information you're looking for. Many will be only somewhat relevant. Many will not even be close.

4. When you see a link you like, simply click the highlighted words and your Web browser will take you to that site.

5. After you look over a site, click the Back button on your Web browser until you get back to Excite. You then can evaluate more pages through other links.

6. When you find a site you really like, go back to Excite and click the text next to the site's link that says More Like This (see Figure 2.2). Excite then will generate a new list that should include more links relevant to your topic.

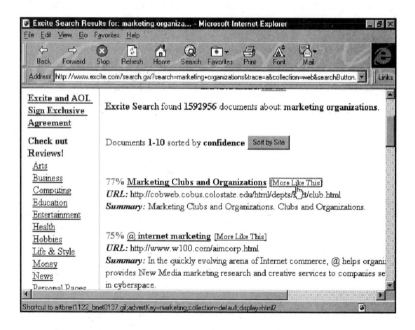

Figure 2.2   When you find a site you like, click More Like This to create a new list of search results. It should contain more relevant sites than the first list.

TIP **Enter Many Keywords** For better search results, list as many keywords as possible in Excite's search entry window. You may want to enter something similar to **marketing advertising organizations associations**. Note that you do not have to enter punctuation or grammatical sentences. In fact, Excite strips out words like **the**, **a**, and **those**. Also be sure to check your spelling. Even a small error can cause you to miss relevant information.

TIP **Searching Proper Names** If you need to look up a proper name such as Bill Gates or Apple Computer, just capitalize the first letters of each word as you normally would. Excite will find only Web pages that contain the terms as proper names.

TIP **Sorting Search Results** Excite initially presents search results sorted by relevance, indicated by the percentage rating. If you want to see a list that shows which sites have the most pages containing your search terms, click the Sort by Site button at the top of the search results page.

Advanced Searching Made Simple

Having too much information can be as bad as having no information. When you're using a search engine, how can you enhance your search results to increase the number of relevant hits while decreasing the number of false hits?

Instead of entering just simple keywords in a search engine, you use keywords with Boolean and proximity operators. You also may want to use wildcard characters. Don't let those terms scare you. Sophisticated search techniques sound more complicated than they are. And once you know how to use them, you will realize they are worth the little extra effort they require.

USING BOOLEAN OPERATORS

Boolean operators are named after the English mathematician George Boole (1815-1864). They are called Boolean operators because they reflect his work in mathematical logic. Sometimes they are called logical operators. They include **AND**, **OR**, and **NOT**. Because they specify the relationship between keywords, you can use them to broaden or narrow a search.

- The **AND** operator narrows a search because it indicates that two or more keywords must be found in the same Web page. For example, if you enter **marketing and organization**, you're telling the search engine that both **marketing** and **organization** must appear on the pages you want the engine to find for you.

- The **OR** operator broadens a search because it indicates that either keyword must be in a page. If you enter **marketing or advertising**, you're telling the search engine to find pages containing either **marketing** or **advertising** or both.

- The **NOT** operator, sometimes expressed as **AND NOT**, narrows a search because it indicates that a keyword must not appear on the pages you want to find. If you enter **marketing not advertising**, you're telling the search engine that you want pages with the word **marketing** on them but you don't want them if they also have the word **advertising**.

These are simple examples, but Boolean operators can help you create complex, precise search strategies—especially on systems that also let you use parentheses to group keywords. For example, you could create a strategy that looks similar to this: **(marketing or advertising) and (organizations or associations) and not consultants**.

What does that mean in regular English? You're telling the search engine that the Web pages you want to find must have either the word **marketing** or **advertising**, and they also must have either the word **organizations** or **associations**, but they cannot have the word **consultants**.

By the way, if you enter just keywords in a search engine without specifying which Boolean operators you want to use, you are still using them. The search engine automatically inserts them for you even though you don't see them on the screen. The reason you want to insert them yourself is because not all search engines use the same default operators. One engine may automatically insert the **OR** operator between your keywords. Another may insert **AND**.

Using Proximity Operators

Proximity operators let you specify how close one of your keywords should be to another in the Web pages you're trying to find.

The most common proximity operator used by Web search engines is **NEAR**, which tells the system that you want one keyword to be within a certain number of words of the other. For example, if you enter **marketing near organizations**, you're telling the search engine that you want **marketing** and **organizations** to be within X words of each other. Some search engines let you determine the value for X. Other systems interpret **near** to mean within a value set by the search engine.

Other proximity operators you may be able to use include WITH, ADJ (short for adjacent), and FOLLOWED BY. All these operators tell the search engine that your first keyword must immediately precede the one that follows it (for example, **marketing with organizations**).

Using Wildcard Characters

Wildcard characters help you find plurals and alternate spellings of your keywords because they let you specify that a letter in a word can be replaced by any other letter or by none at all. For example, if you use the common wildcard character * in the middle of the word **organi*ations** you will retrieve Web pages with the English spelling **organisations** as well as the American spelling **organizations**. If you use a wildcard character at the end of a word (for example, **organization***) you will retrieve pages with both singular and plural forms of the word. You also will retrieve pages with the words **organizational** and **organizationally**.

A Sample Search with AltaVista

AltaVista is a search engine that lets you use wildcard characters and Boolean and proximity operators.

To begin an AltaVista search:

1. Type the URL **http://www.altavista.digital.com/** in your Web browser and press Enter.

2. Click the Advanced button at the top of AltaVista's main screen.

3. In the Selection Criteria window, enter a search statement that includes all the advanced techniques explained in this chapter. In Figure 2.3, the researcher has entered **marketing near (organi*ation* or association*) and not consultant***. (Note: AltaVista interprets NEAR to mean within ten words.) To help rank the results, the researcher has entered **marketing organi*ation* association*** in the Results Ranking Criteria window.

4. After you have filled in both windows, click the Submit Advanced Query button. (You can leave the Start Date and End Date windows empty.)

5. When you receive the search results list, compare it with the one you created with Excite. Because you used advanced search techniques, AltaVista should provide fewer links but they should be, on average, the most relevant ones—though you still may have to visit several sites to find the ones that truly meet your needs (see Figure 2.4).

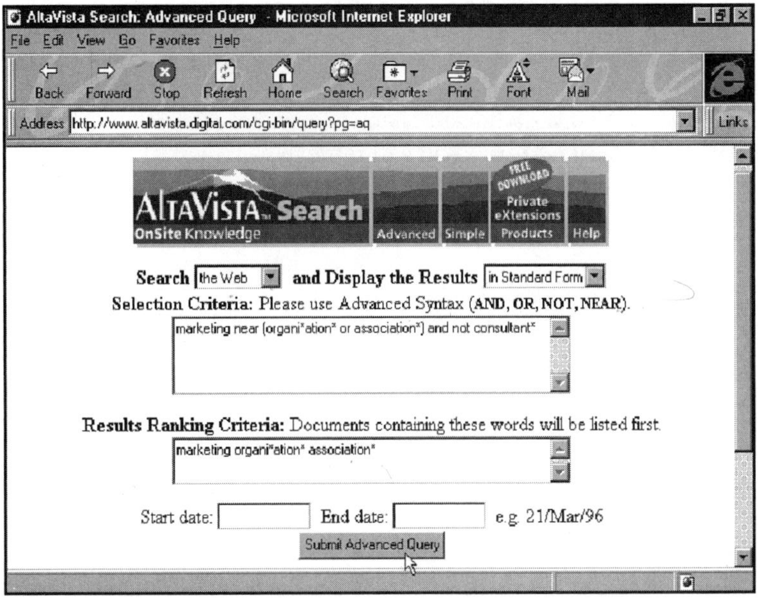

FIGURE 2.3   AltaVista lets you use many advanced search techniques.

Searching Phrases   If you want to search a multi-word phrase in AltaVista, put the phrase in quotation marks. For example, if you put the phrase **"marketing organizations"** in quotation marks, you'll ensure that those two words appear together in the Web pages you're seeking.

Boolean Operators as Keywords   In AltaVista, if you need to use Boolean operators as keywords, place them in quotation marks (for example, **"and"**).

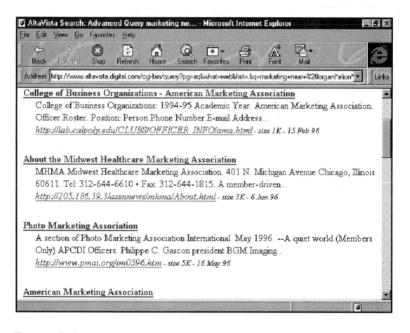

FIGURE 2.4 When you use advanced search techniques in AltaVista, you can produce highly targeted search results.

The Right AltaVista So you point your Web browser to AltaVista, but the screen that appears doesn't look anything like the one in Figure 2.3. What's up? Well, AltaVista may have remodeled its interface since this book was published, but the more likely problem is that you're visiting the wrong AltaVista. Yes, there are two. (As if the Web weren't complex enough.) The URL for one is **http://www.altavista.com**. The other is **http://www.altavista.digital.com/**. If you're looking for the powerful search engine that lets you use advanced techniques, be sure to use the latter URL.

USING OTHER SEARCH ENGINES

No single search engine will meet all information needs. Here are notes on several other sites you may want to try.

- **HotBot (http://www.hotbot.com)** indexes more than 54 million Web sites as well as content in newsgroups.

- **Infoseek (http://www.infoseek.com)** helps you search through more than 1.5 million Web sites as well as newsgroups, company directory listings, e-mail addresses, and Web FAQs (answers to Frequently Asked Questions).

- **Lycos (http://www.lycos.com)** covers 66 million sites. Besides text, you also can search the Web for images and sound files.

- **Magellan (http://www.mckinley.com)** includes numerous categories and subcategories. Magellan also offers a directory of rated and reviewed sites.

- **Webcrawler (http://www.webcrawler.com)** indexes about two million sites. It also offers an extensive selection of Web site reviews.

- **Yahoo! (http://www.yahoo.com)** categorizes about 400,000 sites. Because they are indexed by humans instead of automated technology, you usually will find many high-quality links.

SPECIALIZED SEARCH ENGINES

- **MetaCrawler (http://www.metacrawler.com)** is a metasearch site. That means it lets you perform one search through several other engines at the same time. MetaCrawler helps you search through nine sites, including Excite, Lycos, Open Text Index, and WebCrawler.

- **Inso (http://wizard.inso.com)** is another metasearch engine. This one includes a unique feature that lets you choose from several levels of related terms that can enhance your keyword search.

- **Four11 (http://www.four11.com)** is a White Pages service, which means it helps you find contact information for people. Use 411 to find e-mail addresses and telephone numbers.

- **Deja News (http://www.dejanews.com)** searches more than 20,000 newsgroups. For more information about them, see Lesson 14, "Using Newsgroups to Gather Information."

TIP   **Checking Help Files**   Not all search engines let you use the advanced search techniques described in this lesson. The ones that do may process them in different ways or substitute different operators for the ones explained here (for example, using a minus sign instead of the NOT operator). To learn how to use advanced techniques for any search engine, spend a few minutes in the site's help files. You'll find that it's a good investment of your time because advanced techniques will reduce the amount of irrelevant information you retrieve.

Search Engine Limitations   Most Web search engines do not index pages that require the user to enter a password. That's why you can't find information from, say, newspaper articles available through *The New York Times* site. (But there is another way to find those articles. See Lesson 10, "Using Electronic Newspapers and Magazines.")

In this lesson, you learned how to use Web search engines. In the next lesson, you'll learn how to protect yourself from computer viruses.

Protecting Yourself from Viruses

*In this lesson, you'll learn how to find informa-
tion about computer viruses and download antivirus software.*

What Are Viruses?

According to IBM, there are more than 8,000 known computer
viruses. More than six news ones are created every day.

What are they?

Computer viruses are pieces of software that get into your ma-
chine without your knowledge or permission. Some viruses are
designed to activate relatively harmless programs that just display
messages or play music. Others viruses can cripple your computer
by corrupting programs or erasing your hard drive.

Viruses get into a computer through a segment of software code
that implants itself to one of your executable files and then
spreads from one file to another.

You cannot get a virus simply by browsing the Web. You can get a
virus when you use an infected program you've downloaded from
the Web or an online service. Most online services scan their file
libraries for viruses. Most Web sites are safe, too. But you can't be
too safe when it comes to viruses.

You can help protect yourself by staying up-to-date on virus information and installing antivirus software on your computer.

Monitoring Virus Information

Many Web sites offer basic virus information. Stiller Research, for
example, offers a great deal of background information and virus
news in a simple, straightforward manner (see Figure 3.1).

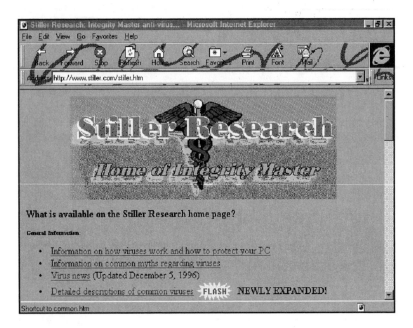

FIGURE 3.1   Stiller Research offers basic virus information.

You can read any of the individual sections simply by clicking the text. The sections contain lengthy, detailed explanations, but they are not too technical, and they offer useful introductory information.

USING ANTIVIRUS SOFTWARE

You can buy antivirus software in retail stores and through mail-order companies. You also can download software from the Web. For example, Stiller Research lets you download a shareware program called Integrity Master.

Shareware   Software you can install, use, and evaluate before you decide to buy it. The program will contain information on how to pay for and register it.

If you want to download Integrity Master:

1. Type the URL **http://www.stiller.com/** in your Web browser's address window and press Enter.

2. Scroll down Stiller Research's main screen until you see the section with the heading Get Integrity Master!

3. Click on any line of text that says Download Integrity Master (see Figure 3.2).

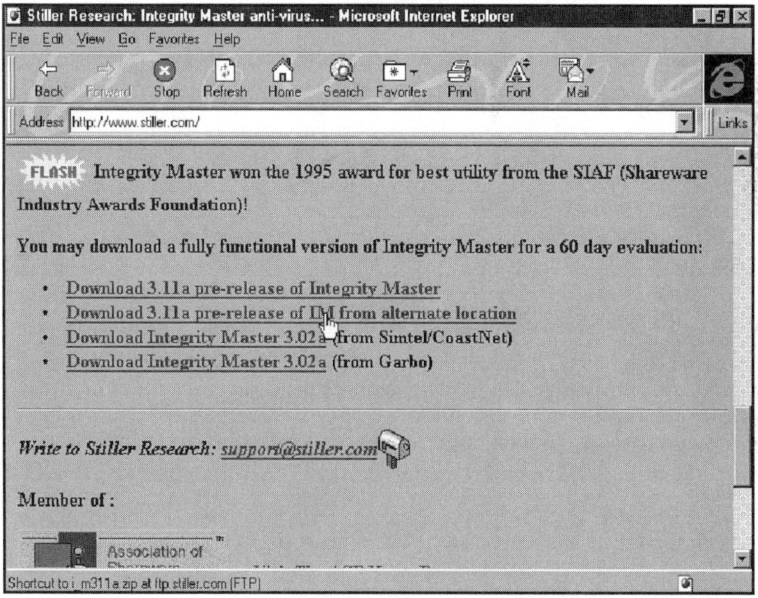

FIGURE 3.2   Stiller Research also lets you download antivirus shareware.

4. Your Web browser may display a dialog box asking whether you want to save the file or open it with a helper application. Select Save.

5. Your browser will display a box asking where you want to store the downloaded file. Select one of your existing folders or create a new one.

6. Integrity Master is delivered as a compressed file. You can open it with file decompression software.

7. After the software has been decompressed, run the program called Setupim.exe. It will walk you through the Integrity Master installation process.

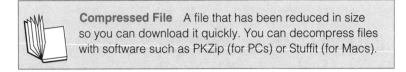

Compressed File   A file that has been reduced in size so you can download it quickly. You can decompress files with software such as PKZip (for PCs) or Stuffit (for Macs).

VISITING OTHER VIRUS SITES

There are many other Web sites you may want to explore. Here's a sampling to get you started:

- **AntiVirus Resources (http://www.hitchhikers. net/av.shtml)** offers extensive news, alerts, basic information, and software. You also can register for automatic e-mail notification of software upgrades.

- **Symantec Antivirus Resource Center (http:// www.symantec.com/avcenter/index.html)** provides alerts and a virus information database. You also can purchase and download copies of the popular programs Norton AntiVirus or Symantec AntiVirus for Macintosh (but you may get them cheaper from a retail store or mail-order company).

- **IBM AntiVirus (http://www.av.ibm.com/current/FrontPage/)** offers virus and hype alerts as well as advice for people who think their computers are infected and a large collection of detailed technical information.

- **Virus Information (http://csrc.ncsl.nist.gov/ virus/)** provides reviews of antivirus software and miscellaneous information from the National Institute of Standards and Technology's Computer Security Research Clearinghouse.

- **The Computer Virus Help Desk (http:// www.indyweb.net/~cvhd)** offers basic information and an extensive selection of links to other virus sites.

MONITORING VIRUS INFORMATION WITH ONLINE SERVICES

Many online services offer their own areas where you can monitor virus information and download software. America Online, for example, offers both a PC Virus Information Center (keyword: **pc virus**) and a Macintosh Virus Information center (keyword: **mac virus**). Both offer basic information, message boards, scheduled real-time chats, and links to antivirus software libraries. (See Lesson 23, "Using Business Resources on America Online," for more information about using America Online.)

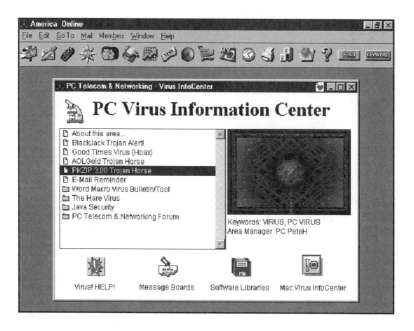

FIGURE 3.3   Many online services offer virus information for their members. For example, America Online's PC Virus Information Center can help you learn how to stay protected.

In this lesson, you learned how to protect yourself against computer viruses. In the next lesson, you'll learn how to find information in Internet libraries.

CHECKING OUT INTERNET LIBRARIES

In this lesson, you'll find our how to use resources in libraries on the Web.

USING THE INTERNET PUBLIC LIBRARY

The Internet Public Library was founded in 1995 during a graduate seminar at the University of Michigan's School of Information and Library Studies. Today, the library has grant funding and a full-time paid staff. IPL includes several sections modeled after a real library, including reference, youth services, and a reading room (see Figure 4.1).

You'll find links to business resources in the reference section. You won't find nearly as many links as you would in a site like Yahoo! (mentioned in Lesson 2, "Searching the Web"). In fact, the entire reference collection contains only about 1,100 items. What you will find, however, is a carefully selected collection of links to high-quality resources in the following business categories.

- Banking
- Business Administration & Management
- Business & Industry
- Consumer Issues & Services
- Economics
- Employment
- Finance
- Insurance

- Labor & Workplace
- Marketing & Advertising
- News
- Non-Profit Organizations
- Statistics
- Stocks
- Trade

These categories are not intended to be comprehensive guides to all relevant sites on the Web. Instead, the links in the categories are carefully selected for inclusion by IPL's librarians. To be selected, a site must be high in useful content and updated consistently. According to IPL's selection policy, the site must be "designed such that any graphics are an attractive complement to the information rather than a flashy distraction from it." In addition, the site should offer a text interface.

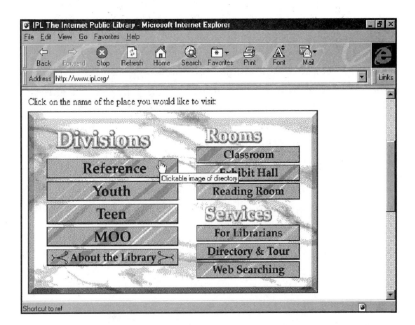

FIGURE 4.1   The Internet Public Library is modeled after a real library.

Text Interface   A Web site that does not include images. Many sites provide both a graphical interface and a text interface because people with slow Internet connections cannot navigate graphical sites efficiently.

BROWSING THE REFERENCE COLLECTION

To check out business information at the Internet Public Library:

1. Type the URL **http://www.ipl.org** in your Web browsers address box and press Enter.

2. Click the Reference button on the main screen (see Figure 4.1).

3. Your Web browser will display an image of the library's reference collection (see Figure 4.2). Clicking any text in the image will take you to that category. For this lesson, click Business & Economics.

4. You will see the Business & Economics subcategories. To browse one, click the name. For example, click the statistics subsection and you will see links to several sites, including the Bureau of Labor Statistics Data and the Census Bureau's Economic Information. Note that each link in the subcategories includes a description of the site and the name of the publisher.

5. To visit a site, click its name.

6. To return to the Internet Public Library, click the Back button on your browser.

7. Some of the library's categories include general resources in addition to the specific ones in the subcategories. Scroll down the main page for the Business & Economics category and you will see several general resources, including The Relocation Salary Calculator and Virtual International Business and Economic Sources (VIBES).

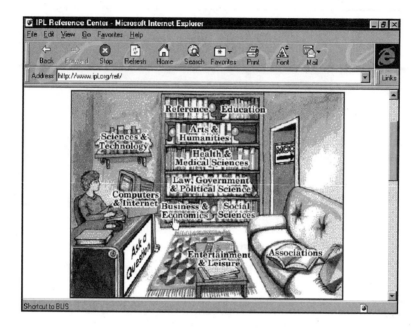

Figure 4.2   The library's reference division covers multiple topics.

8. Scroll to the bottom of the page and you will see that you also can search the library's reference collection. You can search all the categories or just the Business & Economics category.

9. Enter keywords in the search entry window. You usually will get better results if you search with broad terms rather than specific words. In Figure 4.3, the researcher has entered the keywords **international trade**.

10. After you enter your keywords, click the Search button. You will receive a list of links relevant to your keywords. For example, the international trade search will provide links to online resources such as the Census Bureau's Economic Information and the International Business Practices Guide.

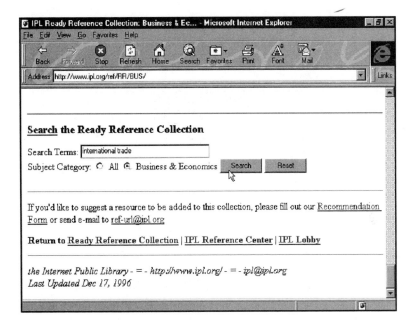

FIGURE 4.3   You can search the Internet Public Library's reference collection.

ASKING A REFERENCE QUESTION

The Internet Public Library also offers a reference desk staffed by full-time librarians and volunteers. To ask a reference question, just click the text that says Ask a Question on the front of the desk on the reference area's main screen (see Figure 4.2). You can enter your question on a simple form. You also can send a question by e-mail.

You usually can expect a reply via e-mail in one or two days. The reply will be a brief, factual answer or a short list of suggested resources for further exploration of your topic. Most of the resources will be available on the Internet, but the list also may include traditional library material.

If you have a big research project, IPL's staff may suggest places you can look for the information you need to get started, but the staff can't do extensive research for you. Also note that IPL's reference service is still in the experimental stage, and the librarians sometimes need to limit the number and type of questions they take. Before you submit a question, check to see if it already has been answered in the list of Frequently Asked Reference Questions.

USING OTHER WEB LIBRARIES

Several other libraries have established a presence on the Web:

- The **Michigan Electronic Library** includes an excellent Business, Economics, and Labor section (**http://mel.lib.mi.us/business/business-index.html**).

- The **Library of Congress (http://www.loc.gov/)** offers numerous resources.

- **St. Joseph County Public Library Servers Database (http://sjcpl.lib.in.us/Databases/PubLibServFind.html)** can help you find Web pages developed by real libraries.

- The **WWW Virtual Library (http://www.w3.org/pub/DataSources/bySubject/Overview.html)** is a massive subject list developed by the World Wide Web Consortium, a project of the MIT Laboratory for Computer Science.

In this lesson, you learned how to access resources in libraries on the Web. In the next lesson, you'll learn how to find company information.

ACCESSING COMPANY INFORMATION

5

In this lesson, you'll find out how to access and use several company information sources.

USING CORPORATE WEB PAGES

It's a sign of the times: Nearly every television, magazine, or newspaper ad includes an URL. That's because hundreds of thousands of companies have created their own Web sites, and more are being developed every day.

Corporate sites can provide a great deal of basic company information. An organization may include not only details about its products and services but also information about its mission, history, strategy, and even hiring practices. Often, you can find information that will help you prepare for a sales call or interview and evaluate potential vendors, suppliers, partners, or takeover targets.

You can find sites for specific companies through any of the Web search engines discussed in Lesson 2, "Searching the Web." You also may want to try NetPartners Company Site Locator. It searches a database of Web addresses from InterNIC, an organization that provides Internet registration services. The database primarily contains U.S. companies.

To search NetPartners Company Site Locator:

1. Enter the URL **http://netpart.com/company/ search.html** in your Web browser's address window and press Enter.

2. Enter a company name in the search entry window. In Figure 5.1, the researcher has entered the name

McKinsey & Company. You can enter a complete or partial name (for example, McKinsey). If you make a mistake, click Clear and start over.

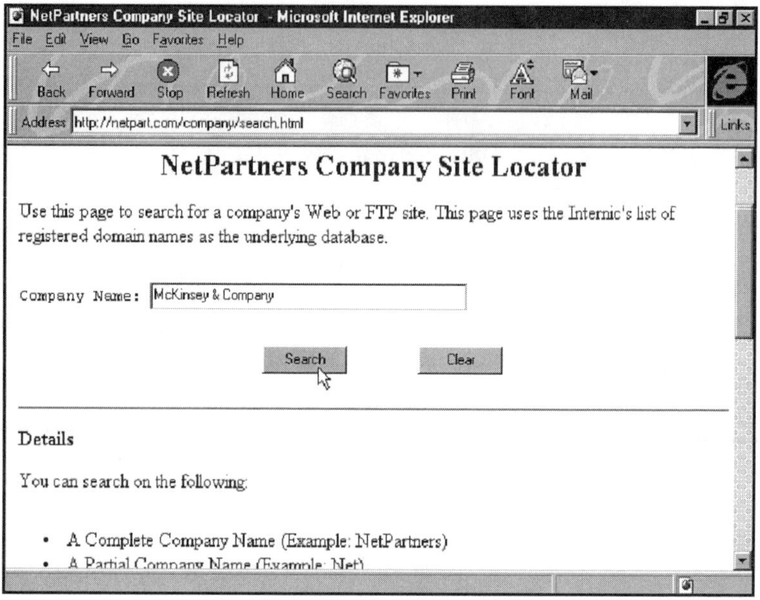

FIGURE 5.1   NetPartners Company Site Locator can help you find corporate Web sites.

3. Click the Search button. If you're searching for a company with a common name, you may have to wait a few minutes.

4. Your search results will include a list of companies matching the name you entered—if they have Web sites registered with InterNIC. You can go directly to a site by clicking its URL in the results list. NetPartners also provides links to company FTP sites.

FTP An acronym for File Transfer Protocol. It's an Internet command for connecting to remote computers and sending and retrieving files from them.

TIP

Company Information Areas When you access a company's Web site, look for a section called "About the Company," "About us," or something similar. That type of section often includes basic company information. Also look for sections that contain a company's news releases. Many organizations now put all their releases online.

ACCESSING COMPANY PROFILES IN ONLINE DATABASES

If you need more information than a company's Web site provides, or if the company you are researching doesn't have a Web site, you may find the information you need in an online database.

FINDING BUSINESS BACKGROUND REPORTS

Dun & Bradstreet offers a database of Business Background Reports on more than ten million U.S. companies of all types and sizes—including many privately held firms. Information on companies worldwide may be added soon.

Business Background Reports provide an overview of a company's history and operations, including details on annual sales, net worth, number of employees, executives, location, facilities, branches, special events, and recent newsworthy items. A sample report is available on the D&B Web site.

After you register, you can search the database with your Web browser. Registering and searching are free, but there is a $20 charge when you order a report. You pay with your credit card through a secure connection and a browser that supports it. D&B requires that you use Microsoft Internet Explorer or Netscape Navigator v1.22N (or a later version).

Secure Connection   A connection to the Internet that uses a security protocol designed to protect the privacy and authenticity of online information (for example, credit card numbers). To use a secure connection, you need a Web browser that supports it. Both Netscape Navigator and Internet Explorer do. To use their security features, you don't need to do anything other than click on a link that says you will begin using a secure connection. Your browser then will display a message that you are about to enter a secure area. When you enter the area, Internet Explorer displays the image of a lock on the browser's status bar. Netscape Navigator displays the image of a whole key instead of broken key. How secure is a secure connection? Most experts agree that it's about as safe as ordering something over the phone with a credit card. To keep up-to-date on fraud alerts, visit the site for the National Fraud Information Center (**http://www.fraud .com**). The site also offers tips for safe shopping on the Web.

To search D&B's database of Business Background Reports:

1. Enter the URL http://www.dnb.com/ in your Web browser's address box and press Enter.

2. On the Dun & Bradstreet main screen, click the icon labeled Not a U.S. Subscriber (unless you have an account with the D&B Dunslink service—this lesson assumes you don't).

3. Click the text that says Business Background Report.

4. Click Begin D&B's Online Access. Your browser will display a notice that you are about to begin viewing pages through a secure connection. Click Yes, you want to continue.

5. D&B's Terms of Use will appear on the screen. Read the terms and click I agree. That will open the registration screen.

6. Register by entering your name, telephone number, e-mail address, and postal address. Be sure to enter the address where you receive your credit card bills. If you have registered before, click Already Registered or Fast Access and enter only your last name and telephone number.

7. When the Company Search screen appears, enter the name and state of the company you are researching (the street address and city are optional). You also can search by telephone number or a company's D-U-Ns number (an identifying number assigned by D&B). In the example in Figure 5.2, the researcher has entered the name McKinsey & Company and the state abbreviation NY.

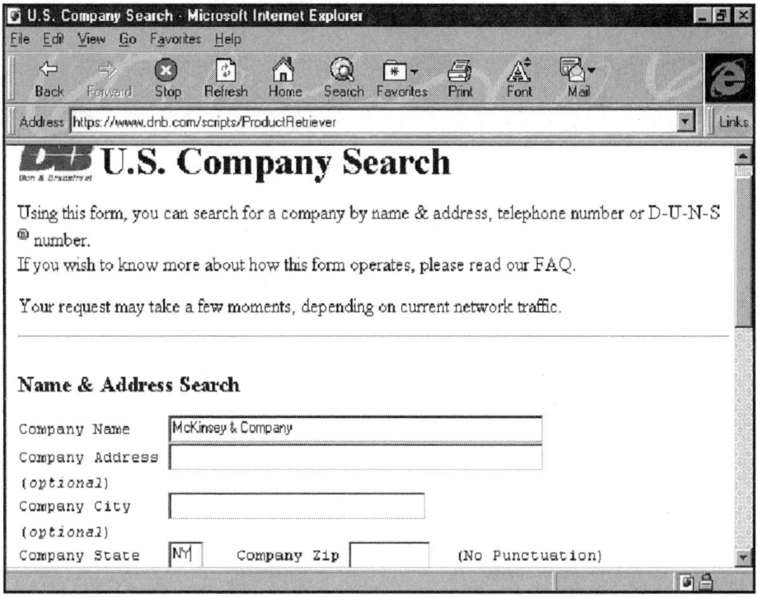

FIGURE 5.2   Dun & Bradstreet provides Business Background Reports for more than ten million U.S. companies.

8. Click the Perform Search button beneath the company state field.

9. A list of companies and their locations will appear on the screen. If the company you're looking for is not listed, try entering a shortened form of the company name and resubmitting the search. When the company you're researching is listed, click the circle beside the company's name and then click Submit.

10. D&B will ask for your credit card billing details, display your total cost, and ask you to confirm your order by clicking the Yes button. The report will be delivered to you directly on the Web. D&B saves purchased reports for three days. You can bookmark a report and retrieve it again during that time. You also can save the report on your own computer (see the next lesson).

- TIP - **Researching Company Branches**   For company branch locations, the Dun & Bradstreet Business Background Reports contain only basic identification information (for example, location, type of industry, top executive, and the headquarters to which the branch reports). Remember that branch locations do not report sales information separately from their headquarters. If you want sales information, request the report for the headquarters location.

Waiting for a Response   When you submit a request to the Dun & Bradstreet system, you may get a response in a few seconds or it may take longer. If you have to wait for what seems like a long time, it does not necessarily mean there is a problem. D&B asks for your patience. Do not cancel your request. If the system does encounter a problem, you will receive an error message.

Dun & Bradstreet also offers a free database called Companies-
Online. It contains information on more than 60,000 U.S. compa-
nies. To access the database, click the CompaniesOnline icon on
D&B's main page (see Figure 5.3).

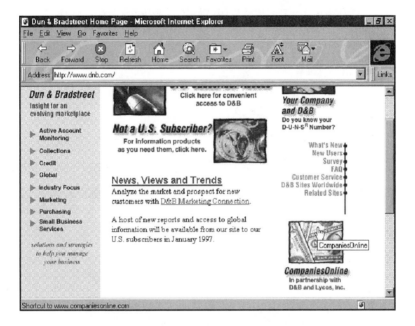

FIGURE 5.3   D&B's CompaniesOnline database helps you find
information on more than 60,000 U.S. companies.

You can search CompaniesOnline through a simple form that
lets you enter search criteria such as company name, state, industry, ticker symbol, URL, industry, annual sales, and number of
employees.

The type of data you can find includes phone number, trade
name, industry, line of business, D-U-Ns number, URL, ownership, ownership structure, ticker symbol, the stock exchange on
which the company is listed, the latest stock quote, and a link
to the complete Business Background Report. If you register for
CompaniesOnline (registration is free, too) you can receive

additional information, including annual sales, number of employees, parent company, e-mail address, and contact name.

SEARCHING HOOVER'S ONLINE

Hoover's Online offers a free database of Company Capsules and a subscription service that lets you download more detailed profiles.

Company Capsules are available for more than 10,000 companies worldwide. To search the database:

1. Enter the URL **http://www.hoovers.com/** in your browser's address window and press Enter.

2. Click the icon in the middle of the screen that says Search for Company Information (see Figure 5.4).

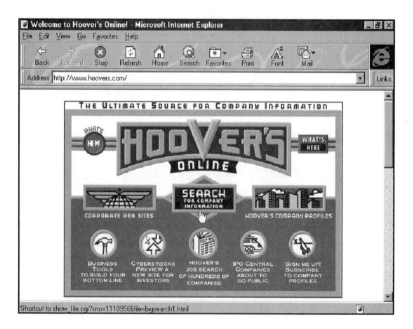

FIGURE 5.4   Hoover's Online offers a free database and a subscription service.

3. A form will appear that lets you search by company name, ticker symbol, location, industry, or sales.

4. After you have entered your search criteria, click the Find button.

5. Your search results will include a brief description of the company and its products as well as contact information, the names of executives, sales, number of employees, and the company's ticker symbol. The capsules also may include a link to the company's Web site and even an online map showing the location of the company's headquarters.

If you need detailed company information often, you may want to subscribe to Hoover's Company Profiles. Covering more than 2,600 firms, the database offers in-depth information on the operations, strategies, histories, financial performance, and products of major public and private companies worldwide.

An individual subscription to Company Profiles costs $9.95 per month for information on up to 100 companies. Special subscription pricing for corporations and academic institutions also is available. For more details, click the Sign me up! icon on the main screen (see Figure 5.4). Hoover's also provides free databases of corporate Web sites and job listings. These databases also are available through icons on the main screen.

Hoover's information is available to members of America Online for no charge besides the regular AOL fees (see Lesson 23, "Using Business Resources on America Online," for additional information about performing business research on America Online).

OTHER COMPANY INFORMATION SOURCES

Wall Street Research Net (**http://www.wsrn.com/**) offers over 140,000 links designed primarily to help investors research actively traded companies and mutual funds. You can find information on more than 16,000 companies listed on U.S. and Canadian stock exchanges. The links will take you to such items as SEC documents, company home pages, annual reports, news releases, stock quotes, graphs, and even audio files. You can search for specific companies by ticker symbol, full or partial name, or an alphabetical index.

Wall Street Research Net also includes links to worldwide economic databases, an interactive economic calendar, market news, general business news, mutual funds, and market research publications.

Some of the links on Wall Street Research Net take you to Yahoo! on the Money (**http://biz.yahoo.com/**), a special section of the Yahoo! site described in Lesson 2, "Searching the Web." Yahoo! on the Money's Company Information area offers company profiles, news, and stock quotes. You can find specific companies through an alphabetical index.

News release databases are another good source of company information. See Lesson 8, "Finding Company and Industry Information in News Releases."

In this lesson, you learned how to access basic company information. In the next lesson, you'll learn how to store the information you find.

SAVING THE INFORMATION YOU FIND

In this lesson, you'll learn how save text and documents you find on the Internet.

SAVING TEXT FILES

If you find a Web page with valuable information, how do you save it so you can use it in a report or another type of business document? It's simple. This lesson illustrates how it works using the results of a Hoover's Company Capsules search in the last lesson.

To save the text on a Web page:

1. Click the File menu on your Web browser.

2. Click Save As (in Netscape) or Save As File (in Internet Explorer—see Figure 6.1).

3. A dialog box will open and ask you where you want to save the file. Select a folder or create a new one.

4. In the File Name box, type a name for the page.

5. Make sure you're saving the file as a text file. In Internet Explorer, click the box at the bottom of the dialog box and change it to read Save as Type: Plain Text (see Figure 6.2). In Netscape Navigator you can use Save File as Type: All Files if you add the .txt extension (for example, Mckinsey.txt).

6. Click Save or OK, depending on your browser. This will save the file as a plain text ASCII file. You will not save any graphics or formatting from the Web page.

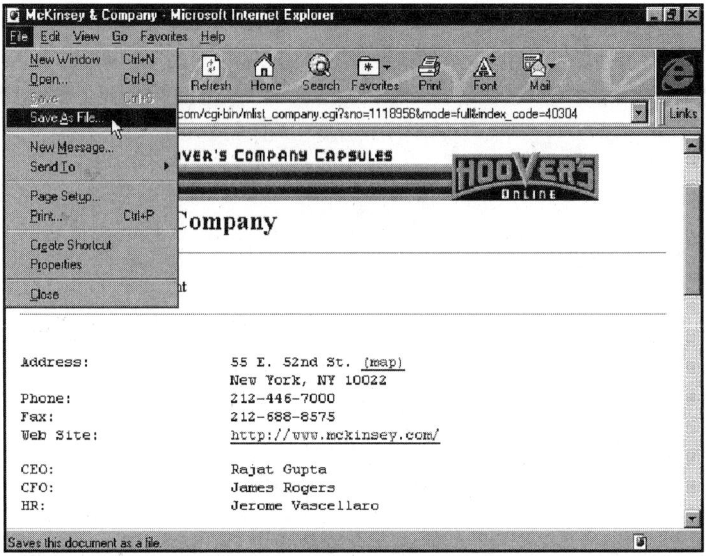

FIGURE 6.1 The Save As File command in Internet Explorer lets you save a Web page.

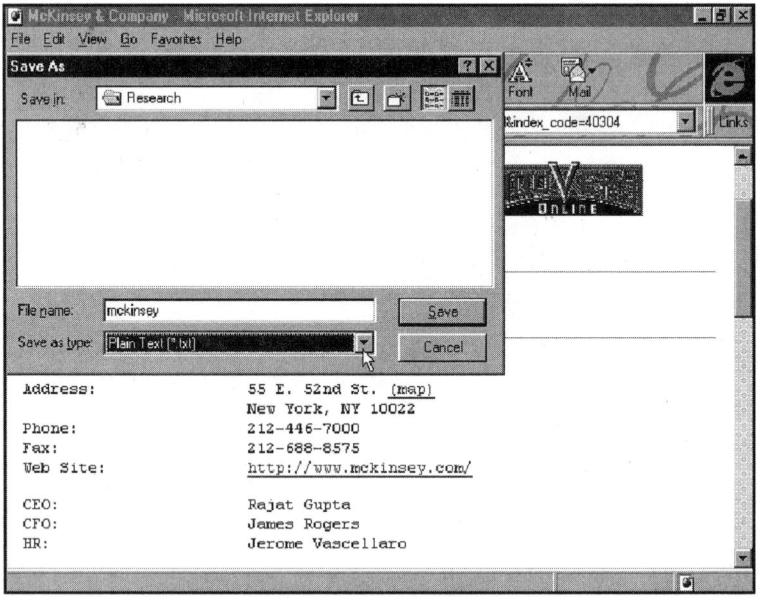

FIGURE 6.2 Make sure you save the Web page as a text file.

Saving Excerpts from Web Pages

What if you don't want to save every bit of text on a page? After all, most pages have extraneous information on them. When you saved the Hoover's Company Capsule, you saved not only the information about McKinsey & Company but also the names of the links near the bottom of the page.

To avoid this, you can copy an excerpt from a page and paste it in a word processing document. Here's how:

1. Select the information you want to copy by clicking on the Web page at the beginning of the text, holding down your left mouse button, and dragging your cursor. When all the text you want to copy is highlighted, release the mouse button. Figure 6.3 shows part of the Hoover's Company Capsule has been highlighted.

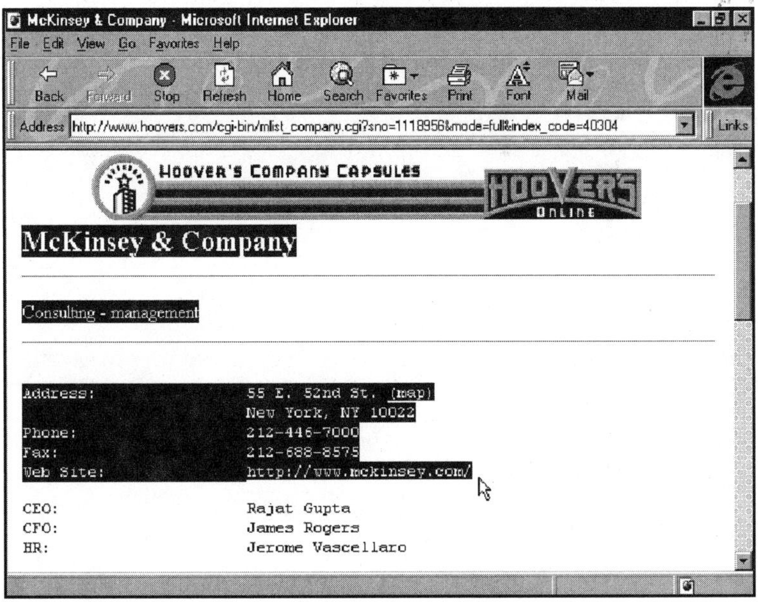

Figure 6.3 Highlighting text lets you save excerpts from Web pages.

2. In your Web browser, click the Edit menu or hold the pointer over the text you've highlighted and press your right mouse button.

3. Click Copy.

4. Open the word processing document where you want to put the information.

5. Click the location in the document where you want to place the excerpt.

6. In your word processor, click the Edit menu or your right mouse button.

7. Click Paste. The text from the Web page will appear in your document.

Text You Can't Save   Sometimes text on a Web page is actually part of an image. This often is true of text in logos, icons, and section headings. This type of text cannot be saved by either method illustrated above. With the second method you can identify text that won't be copied because you won't be able to highlight it with your cursor.

SAVING IMAGES

Besides text, most Web browsers now offer an easy way to save images. Here's how:

1. Position your pointer over the image.

2. Click your right mouse button or, if you're a Mac user, hold the mouse button down.

3. A menu will pop up. Select Save This Image As... or Save Picture as....

4. A dialog box appears. Choose a directory, a name for the file, and a graphic format such as bitmap (.bmp).

5. Click Save. You then can open the image in a graphics program that supports the format in which you saved the file—for example, the Windows Paint program supports bitmap files.

> **A Note About Copyright**   Most organizations don't mind if you copy text or images from their Web pages for your own personal use. If you copy them for any other purpose, the organizations mind very much—and you may be violating copyright law. Sometimes Web developers publish their copyright policies online. If you can't find them and you're uncertain about whether or not you can legally copy part of a Web page, follow the general rule professional researchers have followed for years: When in doubt, get permission.

DOWNLOADING PDF DOCUMENTS

Some Web sites let you download and save documents in prepared formats. The Portable Document Format (PDF) is one of the most popular. For example, you can download PDF tax forms and publications from the IRS Web site (see Lesson 21, "Using Tax and Accounting Resources"). PDF documents are device- and application-independent. That means they can be viewed and printed from any computer—as long as you have the Acrobat Reader software from Adobe Systems, Inc.

To download a free copy of Acrobat Reader:

1. Type the URL http://www.adobe.com/ in your Web browser's address box and press Enter.

2. Scroll down Adobe's home page and click the Get Adobe Reader button.

3. In Adobe's downloading section, click the highlighted word registering in Step 1 (see Figure 6.4).

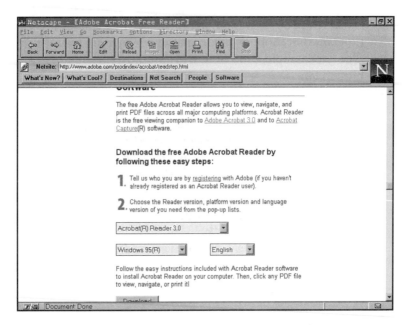

FIGURE 6.4 Downloading a copy of the Adobe Acrobat Reader is free and easy.

4. Adobe will ask for your name, mailing address, phone and fax numbers, and e-mail address. After you type the information into the online form, click the Submit Registration button.

5. Your Web browser will take you back to the screen shown in Figure 6.4. In Step two, choose the platform and language version of Acrobat Reader you need from the pop-up lists.

6. Click the OK button near the bottom of the page.

7. On the download page, click the highlighted text that says DOWNLOAD via HTTP.

8. Your browser may open a dialog box asking if you want to save the file or open it with a helper application. Select Save.

9. Your browser will open another box that asks where you want to put the file. Select a directory or create a new one.

10. When the download is complete, quit your Web browser, run the program you just downloaded, and follow the simple installation instructions on your screen.

Don't Close the Installer If there's a technical problem or interruption while you're downloading the Adobe Acrobat Reader, the installer application will perform a complete uninstall. Therefore, you shouldn't close the installer at the end of the download. It may not be completely finished. Just wait a few seconds and it will close automatically.

HTML Hypertext Markup Language is another document format you may see mentioned on the Web. That's because HTML is the page format used to make up the Web itself. The underlying document is in the plain ASCII text format. To make a Web page, the text is formatted with HTML tags, which are codes that tell your Web browser how to display a page. If you are interested in learning how to create your own Web pages, there are a number of software packages on the market that can help you create HTML documents (for example, Microsoft FrontPage). If you want to see how other Web publishers have created files, you can use the file extension .htm or .html instead of .txt in first part of this lesson. After you save and open the file, you will see the HTML coding.

In this lesson, you learned how to save information you find on the Internet. In the next lesson, you'll learn how to access SEC data.

7

ACCESSING SEC DATA

In this lesson, you'll learn how to access filings with the Securities and Exchange Commission.

SEARCHING THE SEC SITE

EDGAR (Electronic Data Gathering and Retrieval Project) is a database of the disclosure forms publicly traded companies file with the Securities and Exchange Commission.

You can access EDGAR through the SEC's Web site. To search for filings from a specific company:

1. Type the URL **http://www.sec.gov/** in your Web browser's address window and press Enter.

2. On the SEC's home page, click the Edgar database icon (see Figure 7.1)

3. On the introductory page for the database, click the text Search the Edgar Database.

4. You will see a number of search options for a variety of different types of SEC information. One of the easiest ways to search is by clicking Quick Forms Lookup.

5. Using that option, you can enter the specific type of form you are seeking, the specific company, and the date range (see Figure 7.2). After you enter your selections, click the Submit Choices button.

6. Your search results will note the available forms matching your search criteria as well as the date they were filed. To view a form, click the company name in the search results list.

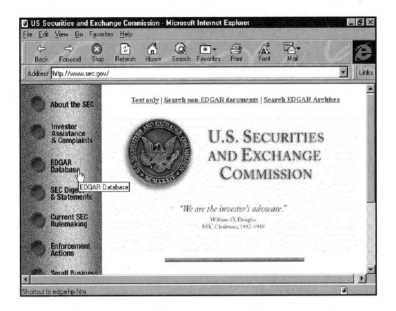

FIGURE 7.1 The SEC's Web site gives you access to a database of SEC filings.

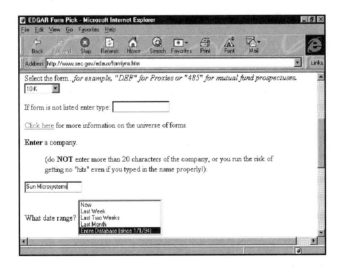

FIGURE 7.2 The Quick Forms Lookup is an easy way to find information on specific companies.

USING THE JAVA APPLET AT THE NYU SITE

The Information Systems Department at The New York University Stern School of Business also maintains an EDGAR site. There you will find an innovative feature called the NYU Stern Java EDGAR Interface. It's a Java applet that creates a scrolling banner of SEC filings on a customizable search screen.

Java   A computer language designed by Sun Microsystems that lets users add animation, moving text, and interactive programs to a Web site.

Applet   A Java program that can be attached to a Web page. When you view the page, you automatically receive and run the applet. To use applets, you need a Java-enabled browser such as the latest Windows 95 versions of Netscape Navigator or Internet Explorer.

To use the Java EDGAR Interface, follow these steps:

1. Type **http://edgar.stern.nyu.edu/** in your Web browser's address window and press Enter.

2. Click the Java Applet Interface icon (see Figure 7.3).

3. On the interface's introductory page, you'll see that you can specify the companies or industries you want to monitor. For this lesson, scroll down the page until you see the section with the heading "Run EDGAR Interface with search by Industry Preference."

4. Click the Save your preference at: Our Server button.

5. Scroll the box labeled Zacks Industry Code and select 044 COMP-SOFTWARE.

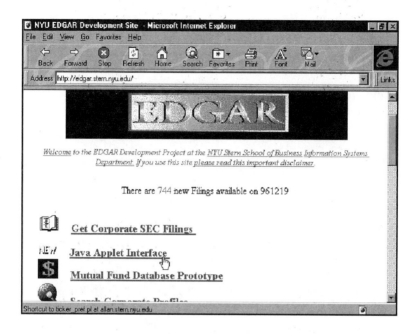

FIGURE 7.3   NYU's Java Applet Interface is a unique feature that facilitates EDGAR searching.

6. Click the Save Your Preferences button.

7. A page will appear that says "Your EDGAR home page:" followed by an URL. Click the URL.

8. In a minute or two, the Edgar Daily Report Ticker will appear on your screen. Look for a box that says Select a Search Tool and Click Go! Click the arrow beside the box and then select the text Latest Filings - by Preference. (Figure 7.4 shows how the box looks after the change.)

9. Click the Go For Search! button.

10. The ticker should change to reflect SEC filings from companies in the software industry. The filings are based on a one-day delayed feed, so you can access all filings from two days ago. Click a specific filing in the ticker to retrieve the filing from NYU's default site or the SEC

server. If you encounter difficulties, switch the selection from "Default Site" to the "SEC Site" or vice versa (see Figure 7.4).

There are a number of other ways to customize the interface. Explore them by clicking buttons and changing settings.

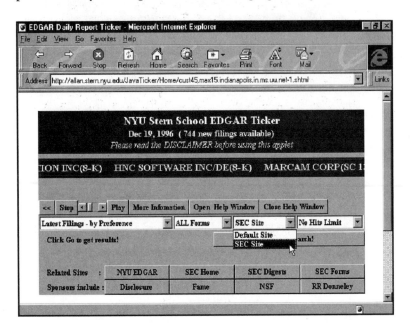

FIGURE 7.4   You can customize the EDGAR Ticker to display the type of SEC information you want to track.

USING DISCLOSURE FOR SEC DATA

Disclosure, one of the sponsors of the NYU site, offers a value-added service called EDGAR ACCESS. For about $5 per month, you can receive up to twenty-five company reports dating back to 1993. The reports can be full-text EDGAR filings or one-page summaries.

You can search the EDGAR ACCESS database by company name, ticker symbol, filing type, filing date, and Standard Industrial Classification Code (SIC). You also can set-up free personalized alerts that notify you, via e-mail, when companies you're interested in file with the SEC.

For more than 5,000 U.S. companies, you can view or print one-page reports that provide annual financial statement information, a list of company officers, top ownership data, earnings estimates, and a list of recent SEC filings.

If you need non-EDGAR filings, or if the filings you get from EDGAR ACCESS are too long to view or print, you can call Disclosure and arrange for delivery via fax, courier, overnight, or regular mail. For more information and to register online, visit the EDGAR ACCESS Web site (**http://edgar.disclosure.com/ea/**). Disclosure offers several other business information services you can explore on the company's home page (**http://edgar.disclosure.com**).

In this lesson, you learned how to access SEC data. In the next lesson, you'll learn how to find company and industry information in news release databases.

FINDING COMPANY AND INDUSTRY INFORMATION IN NEWS RELEASES

In this lesson, you'll learn how to use online news release services.

WHAT'S A NEWS RELEASE DATABASE?

As mentioned in Lesson 5, "Accessing Company Information," many companies are making their news releases available through their own Web sites. But what if you want releases from several companies and you don't want to spend a lot of time visiting individual sites?

You use news release databases. They are created and maintained by organizations that offer electronic distribution of corporate news to the media and the financial community.

PR Newswire and Business Wire are two such organizations. Both offer Web sites with free databases of news releases from companies that subscribe to their services. Both sites are good places to look for announcements of new products, management changes, earnings, dividends, mergers, acquisitions, and joint ventures.

TRACKING COMPANIES AND INDUSTRIES WITH PR NEWSWIRE

PR Newswire's Web site offers a section called Company News On-Call (see Figure 8.1). It contains breaking stories and a one-year archive of press releases issued by hundreds of companies. You can search the database by company name or an alphabetical index.

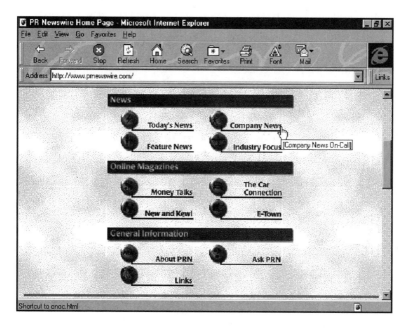

FIGURE 8.1   PR Newswire offers databases of company and industry information.

After you search Company News On-Call, you may see a (+) symbol next to a company name in your search results list. The symbol indicates that the company has more than just press releases available. The additional information may include quarterly reports, a corporate profile, an annual report, a link to the EDGAR database of SEC information, a stock quote, or a link to the company's home page. The search results list also includes a NEW STORY notation next to the names of companies that have issued a news release within the past twenty-four hours.

Searching Company News On-Call is simple and self-explanatory, so this lesson will focus on the Today's New Section to show you how to find information from specific industries and states.

To begin this type of search:

1. Type the URL **http://www.prnewswire.com** in your Web browser's address box and press Enter.

2. Select the Today's News icon from the main screen (see Figure 8.1).

3. When you enter the Today's News section, you'll see that you have three search options:

   - You can search by concept or keyword using a version of the Excite search engine described in Lesson 2, "Searching the Web."

   - You can browse through the most recent 100 releases issued by PR Newswire's member companies.

   - You can search by industry, company name, ticker symbol, or state (see Figure 8.2). Obviously, this option is the one that can help you find information about specific industries or business activities in specific states.

4. To find recent news from a specific industry, simply select it from the list in the pop-up box and press the Search button. You can see that this search option provides a number of other ways to customize your news release search. For example, if you want to find recent releases from all industries in a specific state, select a state name from the box and leave the first box set at All Industries. If you want industry news from a specific state, select a name in both boxes.

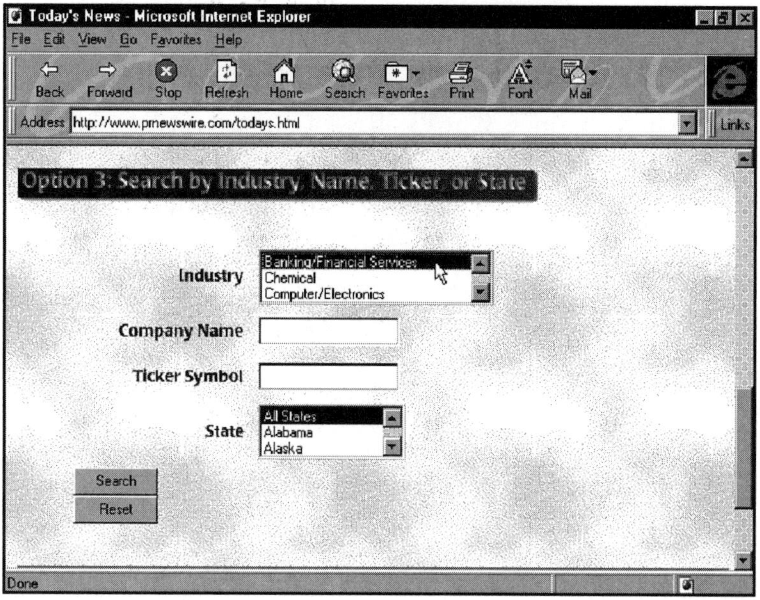

FIGURE 8.2   PR Newswire's Today's News section offers several search options.

You also can find industry information by selecting the Industry Focus icon on PR Newswire's home page (see Figure 8.1). Industry Focus provides news about the automotive, entertainment, healthcare/biotech, government/politics, and technology industries.

PR Newswire also offers links to several other features:

- Money Talks—Financial insights from leading commentators.

- Computer News Daily and Your Health Daily—Links to sites from The New York Times Syndicate.

- Feature News—"How-to" and human-interest stories.

- The Car Connection—An online automotive magazine.

- New and Kewl—Information on innovative gadgets and gizmos.

- E/Town—The Home Electronics Guide

TRACKING COMPANIES AND INDUSTRIES WITH BUSINESS WIRE

To search the Business Wire database of company news:

1. Type the URL **http://www.businesswire.com/** in your Web browser's address window and press Enter.

2. As soon as Business Wire's home page appears on your screen, you'll see that it looks and operates differently than the other Web sites this book has introduced you to. That's because Business Wire uses frames (see Figure 8.3).

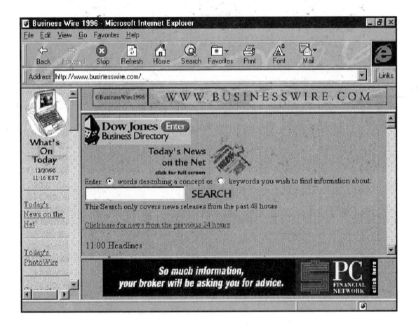

FIGURE 8.3   Business Wire is a frames-based Web.

3. Some people like frames; many do not. If you don't, Business Wire provides an easy way to get rid of them: Scroll down the narrow vertical window on the left side of the screen until you see the text No Frames! near the bottom of the list. Click No Frames and the Business Wire site will revert to the more common Web page layout (see Figure 8.4).

Frames Web sites that use frames divide the screen into multiple areas you can scroll independently. Frames also make it possible to connect with a different Web site through one of the windows. For example, if you click the link to the Dow Jones Business Directory in the large frame shown in Figure 8.3, the Dow Jones site will appear in that frame, but the other frames will stay the same. Most web browsers, like Internet Explorer and Netscape Navigator, support Frames.

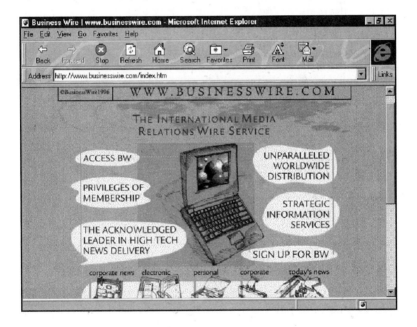

FIGURE 8.4 Business Wire, like many sites that use frames, gives you the option of turning them off.

4. If you're not using frames, click the Corporate News on the Net icon near the bottom of the main screen. If you are using frames, click Corporate News on the Net in the left frame.

5. You can search corporate news through an alphabetical index of company names or by entering keywords. Business Wire also lets you use a version of the Excite search engine to find the type of news releases you're seeking.

6. However you search, your results may include not only news releases but also links to home pages, stock quotes, corporate profiles and histories, descriptions of products and services, and even online photos.

Business Wire offers several other sections with company and industry information. Look for the following icons in the left window (if you're using frames) or on the main screen (if you're not).

- Corporate Profile
- Today's News on the Net (all releases from the past forty-eight hours)
- Today's High Tech News
- Today's Bioscience News
- Retail Reports
- Tradeshow News

For about $15 per month, Business Wire will put the type of news releases you want in your own Web box. How does the site know what type of releases you want? You create a Personal News Profile that indicates the industries and categories in which you're most interested. You can choose from thirty-one industries and ten news categories.

Business Wire will deliver the headlines matching your Profile to your Personal Web Box every hour of a business day. You can open the box any time, click on a headline to read the text, and send the text to yourself via e-mail. A demo of the service is available online.

The news you receive in your box is derived from Business Wire releases and other news sources, including Ziff-Davis Interactive (Daily Wire Highlights), Intell.X/Data Times, First Call Corporate Services, and Knight-Ridder/Tribune Business News.

OTHER NEWS RELEASE SOURCES

Canada NewsWire (http://www.newswire.ca/) offers a database of about 40,000 news releases. You can search by keywords, dates, organizations, ticker symbols, industries, categories, or subjects.

PRESSline (http://www.pressline.com) offers a keyword searchable database of about 20,000 releases from companies worldwide. You also can find out about trade shows in the U.S., Canada, Germany, France, Switzerland, and Austria. The PRESSline Web interface is available in English, French, and German.

In this lesson, you learned how to find company and industry information in news release databases. In the next lesson, you'll find out how to track breaking business news.

TRACKING BREAKING BUSINESS NEWS

In this lesson, you'll learn how to use Web sites that provide breaking news and daily news summaries.

MAKING FRONT PAGE NEWS WITH MSNBC

MSNBC, the cable television and Internet venture from Microsoft and NBC, offers the Commerce Front Page (**http://www. msnbc.com/news/COM_Front.asp**) as part of its online news service. The Commerce page offers direct access to top stories of the hour as well as features, photos, and even audio. You also can find market and economy digests, links to MSNBC affiliates around the U.S., and an international news roundup.

> **Pages don't look right?** MSNBC is designed to look and work best with Internet Explorer. You can view the site with most browsers, but, according to MSNBC, "you may find that some pages don't look quite right." If you have that problem, MSNBC suggests you try resizing your window: "Drag the right side of the window until it lines up with the right edge of the navigation banner at the top of the page. If possible, drag the bottom edge of the window down to create a larger viewing area."

If you use Internet Explorer, you can customize the stock and news ticker beneath the banner on the home page (see Figure 9.1). When you click the customize button, a box will appear that lets you select the stocks and the news categories you want to track. After you close the window by selecting the OK button, click the ticker's update button. You can click any news item in the ticker to get the full story.

FIGURE 9.1   MSNBC provides the Commerce Front Page.

MSNBC also lets you design your own personal front page that will display just the news you're interested in. To get started, follow these steps:

1. Type **http://www.msnbc.com** in your Web browser's address box and press Enter.

2. At the top of the MSNBC page, click PERSONAL FRONT PAGE.

3. A registration form will appear. Enter your name, address, and favorite news sections. You also can add keywords and categories of news you would like to receive (part of

the page is shown in Figure 9.2). You can complete your
personal Web page with stock quotes and sports scores as
well as weather and traffic reports for large cities.

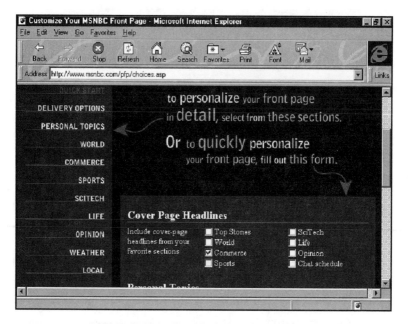

Figure 9.2   MSNBC lets you select the type of news you want
on your Personal Front Page.

4. When you finish filling out the form, click the text near
   the bottom of the page (not shown in Figure 9.2) that
   says save settings and view personal page.

5. If you're not happy with the way your page looks, click
   the Back button on your browser or click the text that
   says **modify your personal page**.

6. After you save your settings, any time you visit the
   MSNBC site, you can click the text PERSONAL FRONT
   PAGE to view your customized news.

READING **MSNBC** NEWS OFFLINE

You also may be interested in MSNBC News Offline. It captures
the news you want to track and delivers it to you when you want
to read it.

You can download a free offline news viewer from the MSNBC
site. One version of the viewer is available for Windows 95 and
NT users who have Internet Explorer. Another version is available
for Netscape Navigator or Internet Explorer users who have Windows 3.1. To download either program, click the Toolkit button
near the bottom of MSNBC's home page. Click Download Instructions for the version you need. Then just follow the on-screen
instructions.

After you've installed News Offline, run the program and it will
guide you step-by-step through the process of setting up your
news delivery choices delivery. They include both categories and
specific topics (see Figure 9.3).

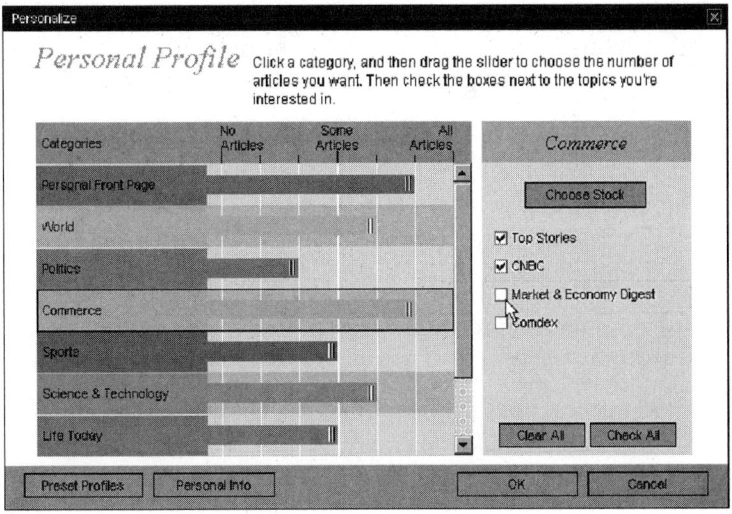

FIGURE **9.3** Choose categories by moving the bars; choose
topics by clicking the checkboxes.

You can update the news pages in MSNBC News Offline whenever you want, or you can set the viewer to automatically log on to the Internet, download information, and then log off at predetermined times. (Note: this is similar to the news services discussed in the next lesson.)

Using MSNBC News Alert

If you have a continuous Internet connection such as a link through a LAN, you may be interested in MSNBC's News Alert. It runs quietly alongside the clock featured in the Windows 95 or Windows NT 4.0 taskbar. You can use it with Internet Explorer or Netscape Navigator. News Alert notifies you of breaking news by either flashing an Alert icon or displaying a headline. It also will notify you of the release of news articles that match your custom news profile.

To get a copy of News Alert, click the Toolkit button near the bottom of the MSNBC cover page. Then click the MSNBC News Alert icon and follow the directions. You can customize News Alert by right-clicking on the News Alert icon in your taskbar and selecting Options. They include the following:

- Specify the time interval News Alert waits before searching for breaking news.

- Type in keywords News Alert will use to find stories you want to read. News Alert's search engine will look for your keywords in article headlines and abstracts.

- Select a method for News Alert to notify you that new stories are waiting.

For more information, click News Alert Frequently Asked Questions in MSNBC's Toolkit area.

At this writing, MSNBC is planning to launch a new Personal Delivery service. It will let you receive a customized MSNBC Web page via e-mail. When you open the e-mail, it will call up your Web browser. You'll be able to read your customized news summary and then jump to the complete text of the stories with a single click. Look in the Toolkit area to get the latest information on the availability of the Personal Delivery service.

Keeping Up-to-Date with CNNfn

CNNfn is an online site from the cable TV broadcaster CNN Financial Network. The site offers several breaking news features. The lead story is displayed in the middle of the home page (see Figure 9.4). Just click the headline to read the complete details.

Figure 9.4 CNNfn provides breaking business news through several innovative features.

In most browsers, the CNNfn home page will automatically update every five minutes. If your browser doesn't support this function, hit Reload often. According to the CNNfn editors, they're constantly adding and updating stories from their New York newsroom as news breaks and markets move.

The area in the upper right corner shows the Dow Jones Industrial Average, NASDAQ, and bond market numbers. Click the links built into the market data area to go to CNNfn's markets page.

If your browser supports Java programs, a news ticker will run directly under the home banner. The ticker scrolls breaking news stories, upcoming interviews, highlights of CNNfn programming, and announcements about the site. Click one of the scrolling items to jump directly to the story. Look for these other features in the menu bars on the left side of the screen:

- **Hot stories**—Includes the day's most important news broken down into sub-sections covering deals, companies, the economy, and biz buzz. Look for Grapevine (CNNfn's "off-kilter business updates") and Hoover's MasterList Plus (the database of company information).

- **Markets**—Gives you access to CNNfn's extensive domestic and international coverage of financial markets.

- **Your money**—Covers many areas of personal finance and individual investing.

- **Digital jam**—Focuses on hardware and software companies, tech stocks and funds, and technological developments.

- **Fn on-air**—A guide to the cable broadcasts.

- **Speak up**—Lets you send e-mail comments and questions.

- **Research it**—Links to reference and business sources on the Web.

- **Briefing**—Links to articles and bulletins posted anywhere on the CNNfn site during the day.

- **Fn to go**—Puts a second small browser window on your screen. The small window will track breaking news and stock market reports while you visit other Web sites. Installing and using fn to go is as simple as clicking an icon, but the feature requires Netscape Navigator 2.0 or higher.

OTHER BUSINESS NEWS SOURCES

- The **Fortune Daily Business Report** provides a twice-daily U.S. and global business news update. You can get the details in both text and audio. **Money Daily**, sponsored by *Money* magazine, offers a business news service that's updated throughout the day. Both the Fortune and Money sites are part of Time Warner's Pathfinder site (**http://www.pathfinder.com**).

- **Newsbytes News Network (http://www.nbnn .com/**) covers the computer, interactive services, and telecommunications industries. Paid subscribers have access to special features, including the Newsbytes archive, which dates from 1983, but a lot of free information is available, too. **Newsbytes Pacifica (http:// www.nb-pacifica.com/welcome.shtml**) focuses on Asia Pacific news. **Newsbytes-J (http://www.at-m.or.jp/~nbj/**) is the Japanese language Newsbytes.

- The **Yahoo! search engine** offers a business news section (**http://www.yahoo.com/headlines /business/**). It features headlines and summaries from the Reuters news service.

- **CNET's News.Com (http://www.news.com/**) focuses on business and high-technology news.

- **Lead Story (http://www.bnet.att.com/leadstory/**), a service of the AT&T Business Network, offers a detailed daily look at a major issue important to business professionals. An archive of past stories is available, too.

- **EBN Interactive (http://www.ebn.co.uk/**) is sponsored by Europe's 24-hour business news channel.

- **Asia Business News Interactive (http://www.abn-online.com/**) offers headlines and Asia market reports.

- **NewsHound (http://www.sjmercury.com/ hound.htm**), created by the Silicon Valley newspaper The San Jose Mercury News, was one of the first automated news services. For about $8.00 per month, News-Hound lets you select up to five subjects you want to track. NewsHound will search for them daily through such sources as Reuters, the Associated Press, PR Newswire, and dozens of journals. Complete stories are delivered via e-mail.

- **Newspage Direct (http://www.newspage.com/ NEWSPAGE/aboutnpd.html)**, from Individual, Inc., provides information from national and international wire services, newspapers, and journals. The information is delivered daily via e-mail for about $7.00 per month.

- **Farcast (http://www.farcast.com)** is a fully customizable clipping service that accesses information from the Associated Press, UPI, PR Newswire, Newsbytes, and Web sites. The clippings are delivered via e-mail. Farcast costs about $10.00 per month.

- **Quote.com (http://www.quote.com)** offers stock quotes and a QNews service that, for about $16.00 per month, delivers information about companies in your portfolio via e-mail.

In this lesson, you learned how to track breaking business news. In the next lesson, you'll learn how to access electronic newspapers and magazines.

Using Electronic Newspapers and Magazines

In this lesson, you'll learn how to find online newspapers and magazines and how to research article archives.

Using Online Newspapers

Many of the best newspapers have created their own Web sites. Some charge subscription fees. Others let you register and read the paper for free, but that may change soon because electronic publications are still trying to determine the best business models for cyberspace.

Some newspapers don't put all their articles online. Others put even more information online than you can find in their printed editions. Still others offer a mixture of both.

The New York Times, for example, provides electronic access to most articles in the printed paper, but they may have different headlines or reflect stylistic changes. In addition, the CyberTimes area features not only the computers and high-tech coverage from the paper but also original columns and articles—marked "CyberTimes Extra"—produced expressly for readers on the Web.

Registering at the *Times* site is free for U.S. readers. Here's how you do it:

1. Type the URL **http://www.nytimes.com** in your Web browser's address window and press Enter.

2. When the *Times* appears on your screen, you'll note the front page is laid out like a traditional paper.

3. Click Register Here and fill in the online form that appears.

4. After you register, you can go to a particular section of the paper by clicking its name in the left column on the front page. To get to the business section, for example, just click Business (see Figure 10.1).

FIGURE 10.1 The Online Version of *The New York Times* looks like a traditional paper, so navigating it is easy.

5. The *Times* online business section will display several headlines. Click one to read the complete article.

6. To access an excellent collection of links to other business resources, click Business Connections: A Guide to the Web. The links are organized by the categories Markets, Investing, Companies, Banking & Finance, Government, Business News, Business Directories, and Miscellany.

An electronic version of *The New York Times* also is available to America Online members. Use the keyword **@times**.

If you register for Netscape's free In-Box Direct service (explained in the last lesson), you can receive New York Times Direct. It lets you select sections from the Web edition of the *Times* to be delivered to your Netscape Mail in-box. You also can create custom profiles that will search the current day's news and deliver headlines linked to relevant articles.

RESEARCHING A NEWSPAPER ARCHIVE

If you click the Search button at the bottom of a *New York Times* screen, you'll have access to thousands of articles from past issues. Another newspaper with an online archive is *The Washington Post*.

Overall, the *Post's* Web site provides articles from the print version of the paper as well as late-breaking stories, comprehensive coverage of Washington-area business and politics, and links to other useful news sites.

At this writing, the site lets you search a two-week archive of articles from the *Post* and the Associated Press. By the time you read this, the *Post* should be offering a newspaper archive dating from 1986.

To search the archive:

1. Type **http://www.washingtonpost.com** in your Web browser's address box and press Enter.

2. On the home page, click the text that says Search. You can find it in the scrollbox at the top of the page or in the left frame under the Need Help? heading.

3. The search page offers an easy-to-use interface complete with search tips (see Figure 10.2). You can enter keywords you want to search for in headlines or in the text of articles. Be sure to enclose multi-word terms in quotation marks (for example, "information technology").

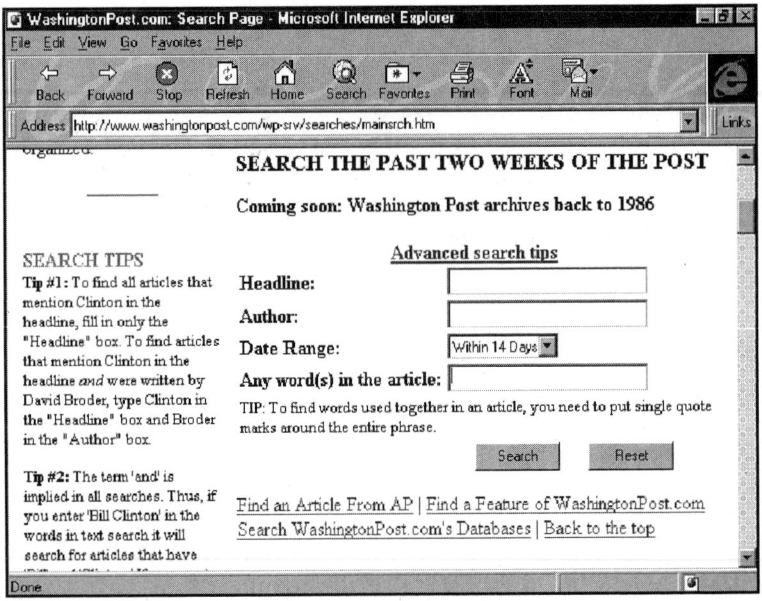

FIGURE 10.2 The online archive of *The Washington Post* will let you search for articles dating back to 1986.

4. The search engine supports the Boolean Operators explained in Lesson 2, "Searching the Web." To see how this engine processes them, click the Advanced search tips.

5. Note that you also can search by author's name and limit the search to a specific time period.

6. After you've made your selections, click the Search button. Your search results will include the headlines of the articles that meet your criteria. Just click a headline to read the complete article.

OTHER ONLINE NEWSPAPERS

The Wall Street Journal Interactive Edition (http:// wsj.com) offers continually updated business news, financial market information, and searchable archives. A Personal Journal feature lets you choose your own news topics and receive a personalized news report. A subscription to the site costs $49 annually. If you subscribe to the print edition of the paper, the interactive edition costs $29 per year.

You can get The Wall Street Journal Interactive Edition Technology Alert through the free Netscape In-Box Direct service noted in the last lesson.

The Los Angeles Times (http://www.latimes.com) includes in-depth profiles of local communities, guides for shoppers and visitors, and detailed entertainment industry news. An archive lets you search for articles dating back to 1990.

Here are the Web addresses of several other notable online papers:

- **The Atlanta Journal-Constitution—http://www.ajc.com/**

- **The Boston Globe—http://www.globe.com/**

- **The Chicago Sun-Times—http://www.suntimes.com/**

- **The Chicago Tribune—http://www.chicago.tribune.com/**

- **The Christian Science Monitor—http://www.csmonitor.com**

- **The Detroit News—http://detnews.com/TDNHOME/tdnhome.htm**

- **The Financial Times—http://www.ft.com/**

- **The Houston Chronicle—http://www.chron.com/**

- **The London Times—http://www.the-times.co.uk/**

- **The Miami Herald—http://www.herald.com/**

- **Philadelphia Online: Inquirer and Daily News—http://www.phillynews.com/**

- **The St. Louis Post-Dispatch—http://www.stlnet.com/**

- **The San Francisco Chronicle—http://
  www.sfgate.com/chronicle/index.shtml**

- **The San Jose Mercury News—http://
  www2.sjmercury.com/index.htm** (Good Morning
  Silicon Valley From Mercury Center, a news service available through In-Box Direct, offers a daily "jumpstart on
  technology, computer, and cybernews.")

- **USA Today—http://www.usatoday.com/** (USA
  Today's In-Box Direct service briefs you on the top news
  stories of the day.)

- **The Washington Times—http://
  www.WashTimes-weekly.com/**

You can find a list of links to other newspapers across the country
and around the world at **Newspapers Online! (http://
www.newspapers.com/)**.

ACCESSING REGIONAL BUSINESS NEWSPAPERS

American City Business Journals is a publisher of 35 city business
weeklies (for example, *Boston Business Journal*, *Dallas Business
Journal*, *San Francisco Business Times*). These newspapers are
especially good sources of information on small, privately held
companies and divisions of large corporations as well as regional
business and economic news.

American City's Web site (**http://www.amcity.com**) includes
columns, a business traveler weather watch, small business information, a sampling of current headlines with links to the publications in which they appear, and a complete list of links to the
individual city journals. In addition, you can search the current
week's news articles and columns from all 35 journals. Click the
text that says Search Here on the home page.

The Crain series of publications is another valuable source of
local and regional information. You can find selected articles,
economic data, and miscellaneous resources at **Crain's New
York Business (http://www.crainsny.com/)**, **Crain's**

Cleveland Business (http://www.crainscleveland.com/), and **Crain's Detroit Business (http://www.crainsdetroit .com/). Crain's Chicago Business** is available to members of America Online (**Keyword: Crains**).

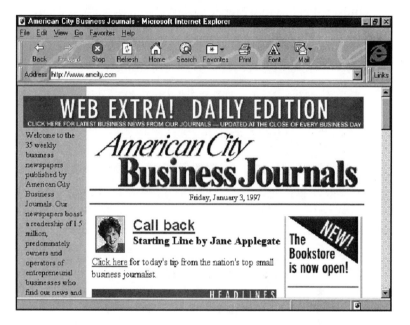

Figure 10.3   American City Business Journals provides links to local business news from across the U.S.

The Yahoo! directory can help you find links to many more regional business newspapers, including some that publish legal notices such as foreclosures and bankruptcies. Use the URL **http://www.yahoo.com**, and then select the following categories: News and Media, Business, Regional, and Newspapers.

Accessing Business Magazines

Like newspapers, many magazines have launched electronic versions of their publications on Web sites. For example, on the *Business Week* site, the latest issue is posted every Thursday night.

Complete U.S. and international editions are available. They include not only text but also graphics, tables, and selected photos.

In addition, you can retrieve articles from a six-year archive. Searching is free. Complete articles cost $2.00 each. Or you can get discounts on orders of multiple articles: 10 for $5.00 or 50 for $20.00. Annual subscription plans are available, too.

To search the *Business Week* archive, follow these steps:

1. Type the URL **http://www.businessweek.com** in your Web browser's address box and press Enter.

2. Click the Archives button (see Figure 10.4).

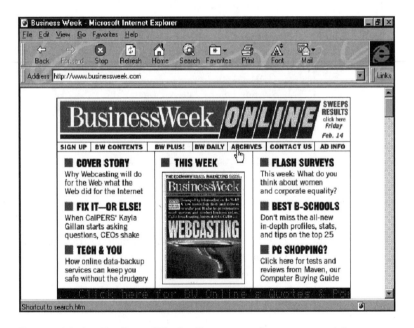

FIGURE 10.4   *Business Week* offers not only current articles but also a six-year archive.

3. On the next page you can browse by groups of cover images or dates, or you can search with keywords. For this lesson, click Search BW.

4. On the *Business Week* search form, enter keywords that describe what you're looking for. Put quotation marks around words you want to appear together (for example, "Dow Jones," "Bill Gates"). You also can enter questions in plain English because *Business Week* provides a natural language search engine. That means it is programmed to understand the rules of English and you can enter such questions as "What is this year's best IPO?" In general, try to keep your questions simple.

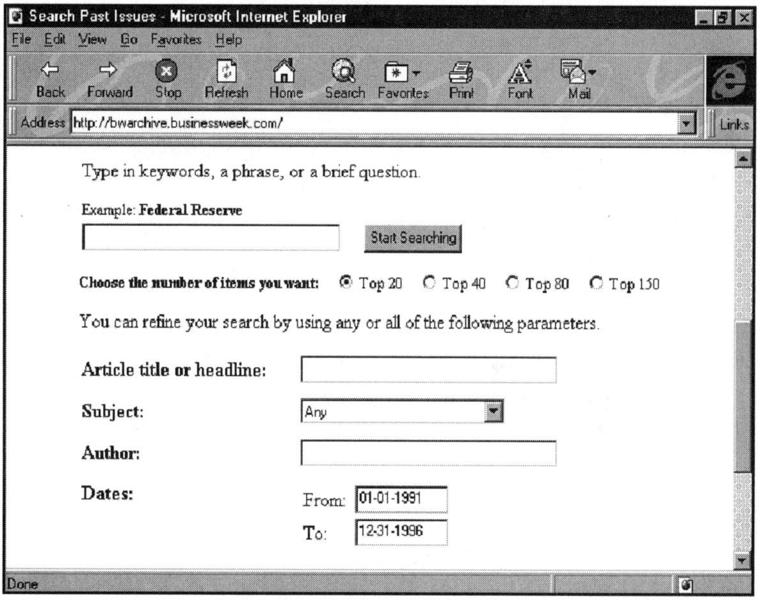

FIGURE 10.5 *Business Week's* search engine offers various search options.

5. The form also lets you choose the number of hits you want to see, search headlines, choose from a list of subjects, specify an author, or limit your search to a specific time period. If you want to search the entire database, enter 01-01-91 for the From date. Enter today's date as the ending date. You also can choose to have your search hits ranked by relevance (the number of times your keywords appear in a story) or by date.

6. After you complete the search form, click the Start Searching button near the top of the page. For each hit, your search results list will include about 40 words from the article. That can help you decide if you want to buy the complete text.

7. To buy an article, click the headline. A form appears that lets you register and enter your credit card information. A secure version of the registration form is available for Netscape Navigator, Microsoft Internet Explorer, and other browsers that support secure connections.

OTHER ONLINE MAGAZINES

Here are the Web address of several other online business publications:

- **Barron's Online—http://www.barrons.com/**
- **Bloomberg Personal Magazine—http://www.bloomberg.com/mag/index.html**
- **The Economist—http://www.economist.com**
- **Euromoney and Worldlink—http://www.emwl.com/**
- **Far Eastern Economic Review—http://www.feer.com/**
- **Forbes—http://www.forbes.com**
- **Fortune—http://pathfinder.com/fortune/**
- **Inc. Online—http://www.inc.com**
- **Investor's Business Daily—http://www.investors.com/**
- **Kiplinger Online—http://kiplinger.com/**
- **Money Online—http://pathfinder.com/money/**
- **Singapore Business Times—http://biztimes.asia1.com/**
- **Worth—http://www.worth.com/**

> **Don't type; link**   You can save yourself the tedium of typing in these Web address if you use the links in the list at *The New York Times* section called Business Connections: A Guide to the Web. See the first part of this article.
>
> — TIP —

USING NEWSPAPER AND MAGAZINE DATABASES

The following sites offer premium databases of newspaper and magazine articles. Many of these services are used by professional business researchers. The companies offering the services are known for providing high-quality information and powerful search systems.

Most of the companies offer articles from hundreds or even thousands of magazines, newspapers, and other publications. Some of the companies make their databases available on the Web. Others offer their own online software. Fees can include per-document charges, subscription costs, or both. Visit the following Web sites for complete details.

- **Carl UnCover (http://www.carl.org/uncover. html/)** is an article delivery service, a table of contents database, and an index to nearly 17,000 periodicals.

- **Dow Jones Business Information Services (http:// bis.dowjones.com/)** offers various news, research, and database services.

- **IBM infoMarket (http://www.infomarket.ibm .com/)** is a Web-based research service that lets you search both the Internet and private databases simultaneously. You can buy information on a per-document basis.

- **IAC InSite (http://www.iac-insite.com)** offers several subscription databases, including Business InSite, Market InSite, Computer InSite, Consumer InSite, and Newsletter InSite.

- **KR BusinessBase (http://www.krinfo.com/products/krbb/krbb.html**) offers online access to more than 6,000 magazines, newspapers, newsletters, and trade journals as well as corporate directories and other database services.

- **LEXIS-NEXIS (http://www.lexis-nexis.com)** offers databases that cover over 4,800 legal information sources and more than 7,100 news and business sources.

- **M.A.I.D Profound (http://www.profound.com/)** offers over 20 million articles, reports, and studies.

- **NewsNet (http://www.newsnet.com/)** offers a database of full-text business and industry news from more than 1,000 newsletters, newswires, and journals.

- **Reuters Business Information (http://www.bizinfo.reuters.com/)** offers several services, including Reuters Business Briefing, which gives you access to over ten years of news from more than 2,000 publications.

- **UMI (http://www.umi.com)** offers many information products and services, including **ProQuest Direct**. It provides summaries and complete articles from more than 4,000 publications.

In this lesson, you learned how to access online newspapers and magazines. In the next lesson, you'll learn how to use competitive intelligence resources.

USING COMPETITIVE INTELLIGENCE RESOURCES

In this lesson, you'll learn how to find and use competitive intelligence information.

WHAT IS COMPETITIVE INTELLIGENCE?

According to *Business Week*, "more and more companies have in-house operations to keep tabs on rivals." At many of those companies, more and more people are turning to the Internet to help with their competitive intelligence activities.

But people who hope this lesson will tell them how to break into corporate computers and ferret out trade secrets are going to be disappointed. That type of data gathering is, of course, unethical and illegal. In October of 1996, President Clinton signed legislation that made industrial espionage a federal crime. It carries penalties of up to fifteen years in jail and a $10 million fine.

Besides, hacking into secret files and other shadowy activities are not what competitive intelligence is about. Instead, CI involves collecting and using public information about rival companies to make effective business decisions.

That's where the Internet can help. It provides access to many potential sources of CI information—sources ranging from online job postings to new product announcements to electronic versions of a company's home town newspaper.

But CI is more than just finding and downloading data. It involves a great deal of analysis and it must be integrated with overall corporate strategies. You get the most benefits when you're working from an intelligence plan. Here again, the Internet can help.

CREATING A CI PLAN WITH ADVICE FROM FULD

Fuld & Co. is a CI consulting firm in Cambridge, Massachusetts. Fuld's Web site, the Competitive Intelligence Guide, offers information for people interested in learning more about CI activities and how they should be performed in their companies.

For example, the section called Developing a CI Strategy provides several interactive resources. To use them:

1. Type the URL **http://www.fuld.com** in your Web browser's address box and press Enter.

2. When Fuld's Web page appears on your screen, click the text in the left frame that says Developing a CI strategy (see Figure 11.1).

FIGURE 11.1   The Competitive Intelligence Guide can help you create a customized CI plan.

3. You will see links to several resources, including the Intelligence Pyramid, which offers basic information on the CI process. The Strategic Intelligence Organizer helps you find out the intelligence you need in various competitive situations. The Corporate Evaluation Questionnaire can help you find out how intelligence-savvy your organization is (it even tabulates a score). For this lesson, select The Strategic Intelligence Organizer.

4. You'll see an interactive table designed to help you focus on specific intelligence activities that will directly benefit your business (see Figure 11.2). Read the information in the grid and click the text that describes a situation similar to your own. You'll receive a list of the types of competitive intelligence you need to deal with the situation.

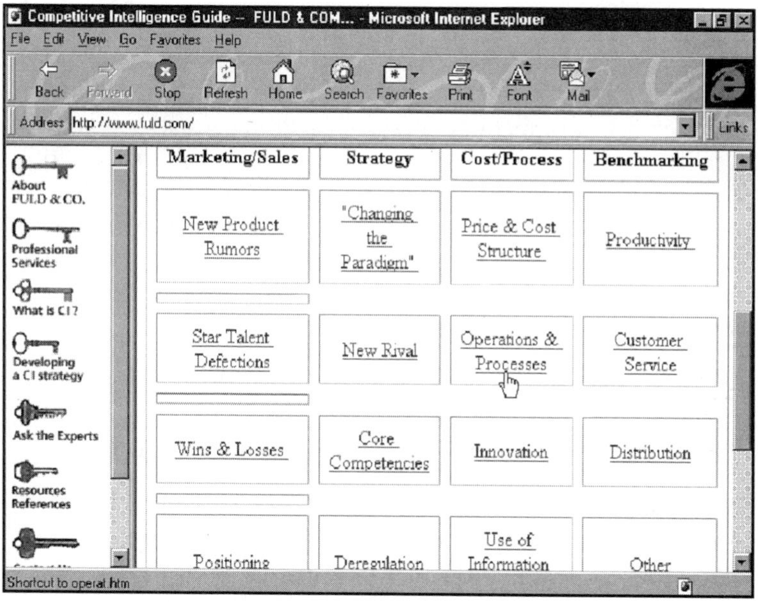

FIGURE 11.2   The Strategic Intelligence Organizer helps you identify the intelligence you need in specific competitive situations.

To find out more about Fuld's services, explore the areas called About Fuld & Co., Professional Services, and Ask the Experts. You'll find links to all these areas in the left frame on the home page. Also look for the Resources and References area, which features the following:

- **The Internet Intelligence Index**—Links to more than 300 CI and related sites.

- **Regional Web Wars**—A survey of more than 100 economic development Web sites.

- **The New Competitor Intelligence**—Excerpts from Leonard Fuld's latest book. You can order a copy online.

- **Thought Leaders**—Articles from CI experts.

FINDING AN EXPERT THROUGH THE SOCIETY OF CI PROFESSIONALS

The Society of Competitive Intelligence Professionals sponsors a Web site that includes online forums and electronic versions of SCIP publications. These resources are designed primarily for CI professionals, but they also may be useful for anyone who is interested in learning more about the CI process. (Please note: Guests are welcome in the forums, but they can post messages only to existing discussions; they can't start new ones.)

SCIP also offers databases that can help you find CI experts and speakers. To use the databases, follow these steps:

1. Type the URL **http://www.scip.org** in your Web browser's address box and press Enter.

2. On the home page, click Expert and Speaker Database (see Figure 11.3).

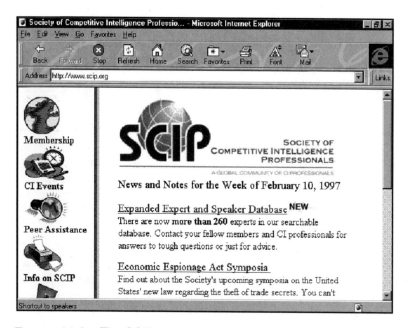

FIGURE 11.3   The SCIP Web site can help you find competitive intelligence experts and speakers.

3. The next page lets you enter several search criteria, including name, city, state, province, country, and/or topics.

4. Click the Search Expert Database button.

5. Your search results will include a list of experts meeting your criteria. For more information about a particular expert, click the checkbox beside his or her name. Then click the Get More Info button at the bottom of the page.

In this lesson, you learned how to use competitive intelligence resources. In the next lesson, you'll learn how to perform market research.

PERFORMING MARKET RESEARCH

In this lesson, you'll learn how to access market research reports and find other marketing-related resources.

RESEARCH AT iMARKET, INC.

iMarket is a Web site that offers several market research information services, including New Business Leads Online, which can help you identify prospects and generate mailing lists. You also can find instant analyses for more than 1,000 industries, a directory of marketing professionals, and information about CD-ROMs for market researchers. Some of the site's services are free; some cost a fee.

To explore iMarket's features, follow these steps:

1. Type the URL **http://www.imarketinc.com** in your Web browser's address box and press Enter.

2. When the home page appears on your screen, click Log on to explore iMarket (see Figure 12.1).

3. On the next page, make up a user name and password. Then click the Continue button.

4. The site will display a registration form. After you enter the required information, click Continue again.

5. The next page offers details on membership options. For this lesson, click Yes, I want to be a basic member.

6. Read the Member Agreement and click the I Accept button.

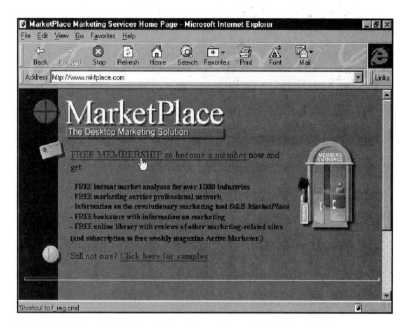

FIGURE 12.1 iMarket offers several services for market researchers.

7. On the next page, click Continue and then reenter your User Name and Password in the pop-up box.

8. On the MarketPlace main menu, you can access several services. For this lesson, select Market Profiles under the Use Online heading.

9. The next page presents a sample Market Profile Report. To create your own, click continue near the top of the page.

10. You'll see a listing of several broad categories. Click the one that contains the industry you're researching. If you don't know which category to select, click Alphabetical Index and look for your industry there. For this lesson, click category I. Services (see Figure 12.2).

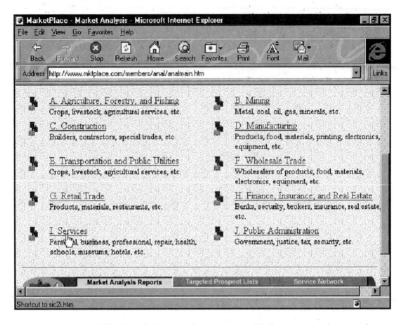

FIGURE 12.2 iMarket lets you browse multiple categories and subcategories to find the industry you want to research.

11. You will see a set of narrower categories. Again, if you don't know which category contains the industry you're researching, you can look for it in the Alphabetical Index. For this example, select category 73 Business Services.

12. You will receive a third set of categories. These should help you narrow your choice to a specific industry. For this lesson, select 7336 Commercial art and graphic design.

13. You will receive a Market Profile that includes information about the size of the market as well as detailed analyses of market share, company size, geography, and specialty.

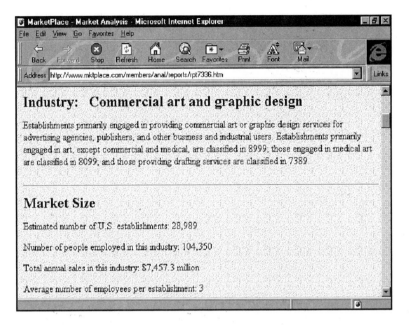

FIGURE 12.3   Market Profiles provide detailed industry analyses.

FINDING MARKETING PROFESSIONALS AND VENDORS

MarketPlace also offers a Marketing Services Network designed to help you find vendors and suppliers who can help fulfill marketing programs.

To use this database, follow these steps:

1. Click the Marketing Services Network button on the MarketPlace main page or on the menu bar on any other page.

2. You'll see a sample Marketing Services Network report. To create your own, click continue.

3. On the next page, click a category that represents the type of marketing services you need (see Figure 12.4).

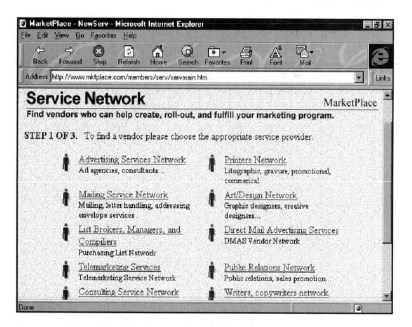

FIGURE 12.4   The Marketing Services Network can help you find marketing professionals in your area.

4. The next page lets you specify the type of vendors you're seeking by clicking the appropriate boxes. You also can enter a three- or five-digit ZIP code for the area in which you want to look for vendors. When you're ready, click the Start Search button.

5. Your search results will include a list of vendors matching the criteria you specified. For additional information, click the boxes next to the names of the vendors and then click Get Detailed Information at the bottom of the page.

OTHER MARKET RESEARCH RESOURCES

- The site sponsored by **American Demographics, Inc. (http://www.demographics.com)** offers several highly useful features, including the ability to search the archives of American Demographics and Marketing Tools magazines.

- The AT&T Business Network offers reviews of several other market research sites. The reviews are part of **Business Bookmarks**, a list of more than 1,000 business sites. To get to the market research reviews, select Business Bookmarks on the home page (**http://www .bnet.att.com/**). Then select the Sales & Marketing category, and finally the Market Research category. Or use the URL **http://www.bnet.att.com/sales/ mkt_research.htm**.

- The **Market Research Center (http://www .asiresearch.com/)** is sponsored by ASI Market Research, a firm that specializes in television commercial advertising research, or copytesting. Features at the Market Research Center include a guide to sites sponsored by major marketers and media companies, links to in-depth information on the market research industry, and an e-mail directory of marketing professionals. ASI also encourages you to send them—via e-mail—any questions you have about market research or copytesting.

- The **Princeton University Survey Research Center (http://www.princeton.edu/~abelson/index .html)** offers links to miscellaneous survey, poll, and research sites (for example, The Gallup Organization and The Pew Research Center for the People and the Press).

- **SimbaNet (http://www.simbanet.com/)** is sponsored by SIMBA Information Inc., which focuses on news, analysis, statistics, and forecasts on developments in the media, marketing, and information businesses. You can access an online newsletter, Cowles/Media Daily, for free.

Other information is available for a fee. Cowles/SIMBA Media Info Network is available to members of America Online (keyword: **CowlesSIMBA**). Features at the AOL site include back issues of newsletters, a user library, and message boards covering media and information.

- The **Investext Group (http://www.investext.com/)** is a firm that specializes in research and analyses of markets, companies, industries, products, and geographic regions.

- **WorldOpinion: The World's Market Research Web Site (http://www2.worldopinion.com/wo/)** offers a Research Resource Directory that lists more than 5,000 organizations from eighty-three countries. You also can find a selection of research findings, the latest research industry news, a collection of journals and newsletters, a list of upcoming conferences, and a comprehensive glossary of research terms.

In this lesson, you learned how to use market research resources. In the next lesson, you'll learn how to use U.S. government Web sites to find demographic data (which, of course, also could be used for market research).

DOWNLOADING DEMOGRAPHIC DATA

In this lesson, you'll learn how to retrieve demographic data from Web sites developed and maintained by the U.S. government.

ACCESSING CENSUS BUREAU INFORMATION

Besides the resources listed in the last lesson, the U.S. government provides a great deal of information that could be used for market research. It could help with such activities as planning new business sites or targeting a direct mail campaign.

The U.S Census Bureau maintains a Web site that offers demographic data on both consumers and businesses. Information is available for various geographic levels, including states, cities, and census tracts. Most of the information was compiled during the 1990 census, but selected data is updated more often.

You can retrieve the bureau's data through a great variety of access tools—from simple keyword search engines to forms to subject search interfaces to interactive maps. You can receive highly targeted and customized demographic reports, and all of them are free (well, actually you've already paid for them through your taxes).

If you need demographic data often, you may want to spend a lot of time exploring the Census Bureau's electronic information services and reading the site's online user manual. To help you get started, this lesson explains an easy way to find demographic details for a specific city.

1. Type the URL **http://www.census.gov** in your Web browser's address box and press Enter.

2. Click the Search button (see Figure 13.1).

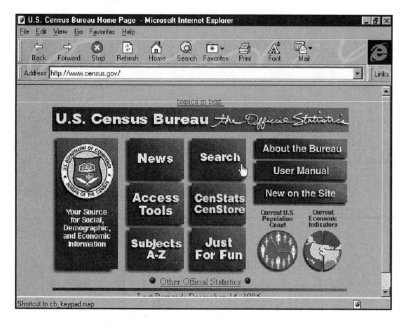

FIGURE 13.1 The Web site sponsored by the U.S. Census Bureau offers several ways to find and download demographic data.

3. You will see various search options, including links to interfaces that let you search by words, place names, or maps. For this lesson, click Place Search.

4. A simple form will appear. You can enter the names of a city and state or a ZIP code. For this example, enter **Saint Petersburg, FL**.

5. Click the Search button.

6. Your search results will include basic details on the city or cities matching you search criteria. (For example, searching Saint Petersburg, FL will retrieve data on both

Saint Petersburg and Saint Petersburg Beach.) For each city, you'll find such basic information as population, latitude, longitude, and zip codes. You also will see links to an online map of the area and the STF1A, STF3A data tables. STF stands for Summary Tape File. STF1 contains information from a 100 percent count of the 1990 census. STF3 contains information from a sample count. For this lesson, click the link to STF3A.

7. You'll see a long form that lets you customize the type of demographic report you want to receive (see Figure 13.2). For this example, scroll down the list and click the following boxes: P80. HOUSEHOLD INCOME IN 1989, P80A. MEDIAN HOUSEHOLD INCOME IN 1989, and P81. AGGREGATE HOUSEHOLD INCOME IN 1989.

8. Scroll back to the top of the page and click the Submit button.

9. On the next page, select to retrieve data in the HTML format. Then click Submit. Your search results will include three tables with the demographic data you specified.

TIP

Searching Web Pages   When you're viewing a Web page with a lot of text on it, you may want to quickly find bits of information without reading the entire page. For example, if you're viewing the Census Bureau page shown in Figure 13.2, you may want to jump to the parts of the form that mention income. You can do this with most Web browsers by clicking Edit on the menu bar and then clicking Find on This Page. A window will open, and you can type in the words you want to find on the page you're viewing. If you search for the word "income" on the Census Bureau page, your browser will jump to the boxes mentioned in Step 7 of the previous section.

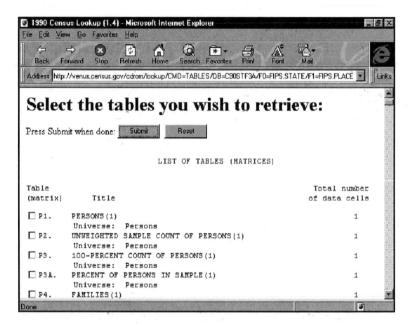

Figure 13.2 Click the boxes that specify the type of demographic information you want.

> **TIP**
>
> **Using the Statistical Abstract** Some of the Census Bureau's most frequently requested information is available in the Statistical Abstract (**http://www.census.gov/stat_abstract/**). You can find a brief summary of key U.S. statistics, state rankings for a range of categories, demographic profiles of states and counties, and monthly economic indicators. The indicators are available for retail trade, wholesale trade, home sales, home starts, manufacturing, GDP, and industrial production.

ACCESSING THE U.S. BUREAU OF LABOR STATISTICS

The Bureau of Labor Statistics provides extensive national and regional information on labor and business. You can find data on employment, industry growth, productivity, and the overall U.S. economy. You also can find the consumer price index and the product price index.

Like the Census Bureau's site, the one sponsored by the Bureau of Labor Statistics offers many different types of reports and several search options. This section focuses on an easy way to find regional employment data. To begin:

1. Type the URL **http://www.bls.gov/** in your Web browser's address box and press Enter.

2. On the home page, you'll see several icons. If you choose the Data icon, you can search for statistics through several forms-based interfaces. For this section, click the Regional Information icon; it will let you access data through an interactive map (see Figure 13.3).

3. After you click the region you're interested in, a page will appear with several more icons. Click the one labeled Most Requested Series.

4. You'll see a form that lets you specify the type of data you want to retrieve (for example, unemployment rates for a specific state). Click the boxes next to the text that describes the data you want.

5. Near the bottom of the page, select the range of years you would like to search (see Figure 13.4).

6. Under the Format heading, select the way you want the data to be displayed.

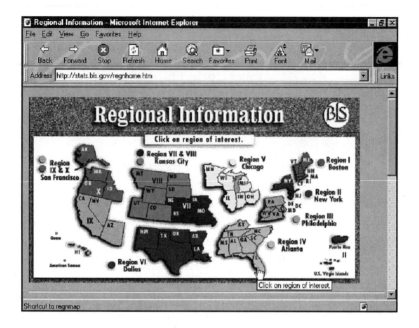

FIGURE 13.3   The Bureau of Labor Statistics helps you find regional information through an electronic map.

7. Under HTML Tables, select Yes if your browser supports online tables. You can leave the other options set at the defaults. (Click the highlighted words for more information about those options.)

8. Click the Retrieve data button. Your search results will include columns or tables of data for each report you requested.

TIP

Finding Consumer Surveys   The Bureau of Labor Statistics' Consumer Expenditures Surveys are reports many business researchers need. You can jump directly to information on how to get consumer expenditure data with the URL **http://stats.bls.gov/csxhome.htm**.

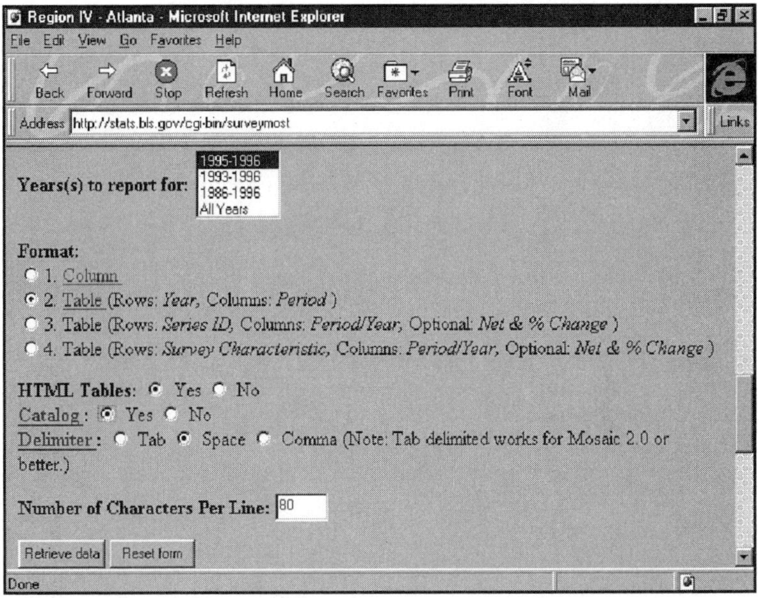

FIGURE 13.4   The Bureau of Labor Statistics lets you customize your search results.

OTHER STATISTICAL RESOURCES

- The Bureau of Economic Analysis (**http://www .bea.doc.gov/**) offers a large collection of economic data. Some of it is available in the Adobe Acrobat Portable Document Format (see Lesson 6, "Saving the Information You Find").

- STAT-USA (**http://www.stat-usa.gov**) integrates several federal data sources into searchable databases. For more information about STAT-USA, see Lesson 22, "Finding International Trade Data."

In this lesson, you learned how to use online sources of demographic data. In the next lesson, you'll learn how to use Internet newsgroups.

14

USING NEWSGROUPS TO GATHER INFORMATION

In this lesson, you'll learn how to participate in Internet newsgroups. You'll also learn how to gather information from them using search engines on the Web.

WHAT ARE NEWSGROUPS?

The term newsgroup is something of a misnomer. Newsgroups actually are electronic message boards that let you read comments from others and post your own.

Developed by Duke University graduate students in 1979, newsgroups are primarily text-based forums that predate the Web. They often are called Usenet (User's Network) groups because Usenet is the system that hosts most newsgroups.

Reliable statistics about the Internet are notoriously difficult to ascertain, but most estimates of the number of newsgroups put the figure at about 22,000. Most estimates of the number of newsgroup users put the figure at about twenty-four million people worldwide.

There's a newsgroup for virtually any topic you can think of—from science to computers to the group called alt.barney. dinosaur.die.die.die.

There also are several newsgroups where you can find discussions of business issues. Here's a sampling:

alt.business

alt.business.misc

alt.business.home.pc

alt.business.import-export

alt.business.franchise

alt.business.misc

alt.business.multi-level

biz.general

biz.misc

biz.marketplace.international

misc.entrepreneur

misc.entrepreneur.moderated

Moderated Newsgroup   Newsgroups that are monitored by their organizers to help eliminate off-topic messages, scam artists (see below), and flames (insults to other newsgroup users).

Avoiding Scams   Be wary of any company or anyone on the Internet that promises to help you make a lot of money. Newsgroups are notorious hosts of unsolicited advertising for pyramid scams and other get-rich-quick schemes. To protect yourself, never give out credit card, bank account, or even telephone numbers in a newsgroup or through e-mail to someone you meet in a newsgroup.

USING A NEWSREADER

You need a browser to access the Web; similarly, you need a newsreader to access newsgroups. Netscape Navigator, Internet

Explorer, and the software you use with most online services include built-in newsreaders. If you use an Internet Access Provider,
the ISP may have given you one.

This lesson shows you how to use the newsreading capabilities of
American Online. You also will find information on a powerful
newsreader you can download from the Internet to use with an
ISP. Finally, this lesson focuses on a Web site that can help you
find newsgroup information regardless of which type of Internet
access you have.

PARTICIPATING IN NEWSGROUPS VIA AMERICA ONLINE

To use AOL's built-in newsgroup program, follow these steps:

1. Click Internet Connection on the Channels display, and
   then click the Newsgroups icon. Or click the Keyword
   button on the main screen, type **Usenet** or **Newsgroups**, and click the Go button.

2. Before you start exploring groups, you may want to read
   the files listed in the scrollbox at the left of the newsgroup window (see Figure 14.1). These files contain basic
   information about using newsgroups. To read one,
   double-click the file name.

3. To browse newsgroups, click the Read My Newsgroups
   button. A window will open that shows the newsgroups
   AOL already has subscribed you to. They cover computer
   topics and a few general-interest subjects.

4. To open a newsgroup, double-click its name in the
   window.

5. You'll see a list of messages. Scan it to find a topic of
   interest. When you do, double-click the name of the
   message. The content will be displayed in a window
   (see Figure 14.2).

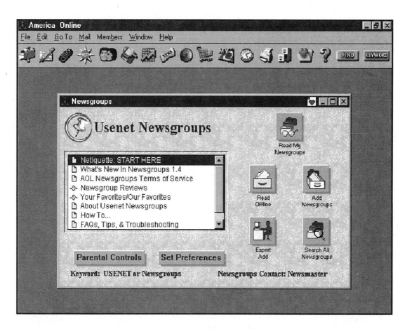

FIGURE 14.1   America Online offers a built-in newsreading program.

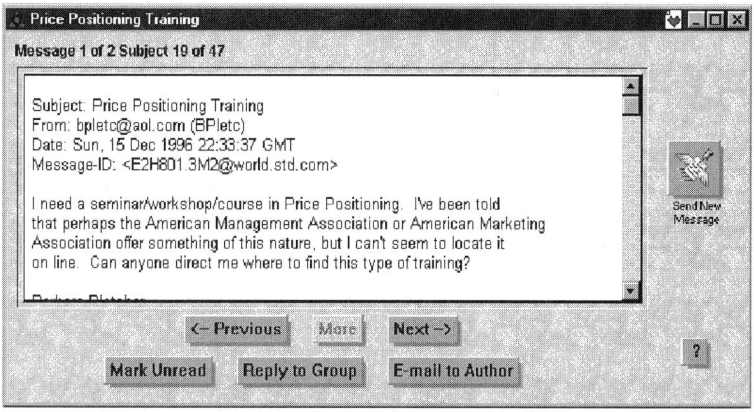

FIGURE 14.2   This message, taken from a business newsgroup, shows how people use groups to find answers to specific questions.

The buttons on AOL's newsreader can help you navigate and reply to newsgroup messages:

- **Previous**—Takes you to the message before the one you're viewing.

- **More**—Displays more of a long message.

- **Next**—Takes you to the message after the one you're viewing.

- **Mark Unread**—After you read a message, AOL won't display it again. If you think you may want to read a message again, click Mark Unread so it won't be hidden.

- **Reply to Group**—Lets you post a response to a newsgroup message.

- **E-mail to Author**—Lets you send e-mail to the author of a message. Your e-mail will not become part of the newsgroup.

- **?**—Opens the AOL helps files.

- **Send New Message**—Lets you start a new topic in a newsgroup.

ADDING NEWSGROUPS IN AOL

AOL initially subscribes you to about a dozen groups. Subscribing to others is easy.

1. Click the Expert Add button on the main Usenet Newsgroups window (see Figure 14.1).

2. In the box that appears (Figure 14.3), type the name of a newsgroup.

3. Click the Add button. The newsgroup will appear in your list the next time you open Read My Newsgroups.

Another way to add newsgroups in AOL is by using the Add Newsgroups button on the Usenet Newsgroups window

(Figure 14.1). It lets you browse categories of newsgroups, topics, and messages. If you find a group you like, just click the Add button.

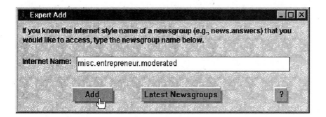

FIGURE 14.3   AOL offers an easy way to subscribe to newsgroups.

> **TIP**   **Finding Newsgroups Names**   To find the names of newsgroups you may be interested in, click the Search All Newsgroups button on AOL's main Usenet Newsgroups window (Figure 14.1). You can use a simple keyword search engine to find groups on particular topics. For example, you'll be able to find several groups simply by searching with the keyword **business**.

DOWNLOADING NEWSREADERS FROM THE INTERNET

If you access the Internet through an ISP, you can download and use sophisticated newsreading programs. For example, Forte, Inc. (**http://www.forteinc.com**) offers a freeware version of its Agent newsreader for Windows. To get a copy:

1. Type the URL **http://www.forteinc.com/getfa/download.htm** in your Web browser's address window and press Enter.

2. Click a download site for your geographic location from either the Windows 95/NT or the Windows 3.1 table.

3. Your browser may open a window asking if you want to save the file or open it with a helper application. Select Save.

4. When the download is complete, scroll to the top of the Forte download page and click Free Agent Installation. You'll receive detailed instructions for installing the software.

With Free Agent, you'll be able to use several powerful features, including the following:

- **Browsing**—You can quickly sample newsgroups before you subscribe to them.

- **Online/offline operation**—In offline mode, Free Agent briefly connects to the Internet to get article headers. You can browse the headers offline and mark the ones that look interesting. Then Free Agent will go online again to quickly retrieve the marked articles.

- **Multitasking**—The software lets you perform several online tasks at once. For example, you could download long articles while you continue to browse a newsgroup.

- **Configurable multi-pane windows**—Free Agent, like most newsreaders, includes a window that displays a list of groups. Clicking a group name will show a list of posted messages in another window. Clicking a message will display its content in a third window. Free Agent lets you resize and rearrange the window layout.

- **Images and binary attachments**—You can post and receive messages with binary attachments. If the attachment is an image, you can view it in the newsreader.

Besides Free Agent, several other newsreaders are available through the Internet. For example, Trumpet Newsreader for Windows is a favorite among newsgroup veterans. Download a copy from **http://www.trumpet.com**. Newswatcher is a popular freeware newsreader for Macintosh. You can find it at **http://www.continuum.net/continuum/downloads/mac/news.html**.

> **Know Your News Server**   Most newsreaders that are not part of an online service such as AOL require that you enter the name of your Internet Service Provider's news server in the newsreader's configuration menu. Contact your ISP if you need help.

SEARCHING NEWSGROUP CONTENT

Several of the Web search engines discussed in Lesson 2, "Searching the Web," (for example, Excite, AltaVista, HotBot, Infoseek) let you search newsgroups in addition to Web pages. Because newsgroup search engines archive postings from the groups they cover, you can find messages that already have been deleted from the groups.

A search engine designed specifically for newsgroup content is called Deja News. It can help you find information in more than 15,000 groups.

Deja News offers both a Quick Search and a Power Search. Quick Search lets you use keywords to find matches in newsgroup postings made during the past several weeks. To use Quick Search, just type your keywords in the first window on the Deja News home page (see Figure 14.4).

Power Search helps you find older newsgroup messages. It also lets you use more sophisticated search strategies. To perform a Power Search, follow these steps:

1. Type the URL **http://www.dejanews.com/** in your Web browser's address box and press Enter.

2. Click the Power Search icon on the Deja News home page (see Figure 14.4).

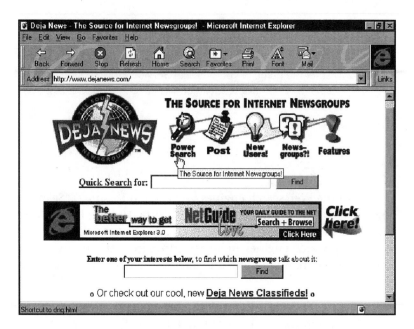

FIGURE 14.4   Deja News is a search engine on the Web that helps you find newsgroup content.

3. On the Power Search page, type your keywords in the search entry window. Deja News supports the Boolean, proximity, and wildcard searching discussed in Lesson 2. To see how Deja News processes advanced search techniques, click Search For: beside the search entry box.

4. Click CREATE A QUERY FILTER on the Power Search page. You'll see a form that will help you create a subset of newsgroup messages likely to contain the type of information you're seeking. You create the subset by limiting Deja News' entire newsgroup database to just the messages in specific newsgroups, those posted on specific dates, those from specific authors, or those focusing on specific subjects. If you need help, click Show expanded Query Filter form with examples. Or click any of the highlighted text beside the search entry windows.

5. After you've made your selections on the query filter page, click the Create Filter button.

6. Deja News will take you back to the Power Search page, but it now will include the selections you made in the Query Filter.

7. Scroll down the page to the Search Options section. It lets you customize your search and the results you'll receive according to a number of criteria, including whether you want the search engine to find all or any of your keywords, whether you want detailed or concise search results, and how you want the results sorted. Again, if you need help, click any of the highlighted words next to the search entry windows.

8. After you make your selections, scroll back to the top of the page and click the Find button. Your search results include a list of messages matching your search criteria.

9. To read a message, click its name. Depending on your Search Option selections, your results may include such details as the date each message was posted, the newsgroup where it was posted, and the e-mail address of the author.

10. If you click the author's address, you'll see an Author Profile. It shows a summary of how many times the author has posted to various newsgroups. It's a good way to find out about a person's interests and areas of expertise.

Deja News also includes a search engine that can help you find the names of newsgroups focusing on topics of interest. Just enter your keywords in the second search entry window on the main page (see Figure 14.4). If you want to learn more about newsgroups in general, click the Newsgroups?! icon at the top of the page.

In this lesson, you learned how to use Internet newsgroups. In the next lesson, you'll learn how to find industry and trade group information.

USING INDUSTRY AND TRADE GROUP INFORMATION

In this lesson, you'll learn how to find Web sites sponsored by industry and trade groups.

USING ASSOCIATION SITES AS INFORMATION SOURCES

Trade associations can be excellent sources of information. Associations with Web sites often make much of their information available at your desktop.

Many association sites provide not only membership details and announcements but also industry overviews, reports, member directories, conference schedules, breaking business news, searchable databases, or electronic versions of journals, newsletters, and news releases.

For example, The American Egg Board (**http://www.aeb.org/**) offers resources ranging from egg industry statistics to an "Eggcyclopedia." The Internet Professional Publishers Association (**http://www.ippa.org/**), an association of graphics and design agencies involved in Web publishing, offers information about and links to sites the association has deemed visually excellent. The American Management Association (**http://www.amanet .org/**) offers AMANet News, a monthly electronic newsletter that covers a broad spectrum of business-related topics and includes links to AMA Publications and Research Reports.

Obviously, many associations provide valuable resources for business researchers. But how do you find sites for specific organizations?

Searching the Directory of the ASAE

The American Society of Association Executives is, obviously, an association of association directors. ASAE's Web site offers an online directory with links to more than 1,400 other association sites. To search the directory, follow these steps:

1. Type the URL **http://www.asaenet.org/** in your Web browser's address box and press Enter.

2. On the ASAE's home page, click the Gateway to Associations icon (see Figure 15.1).

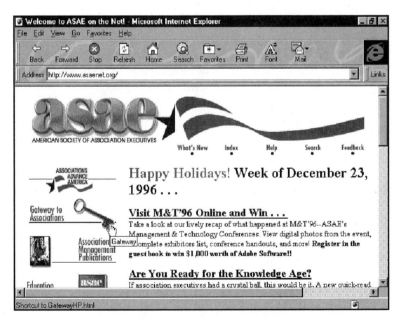

Figure 15.1 The ASAE provides an online directory to 1,400 association Web sites.

3. On the Gateway to Associations page, click Directory of Member Associations On-line.

4. The next page includes a simple keyword search engine. Note that if you use multi-word terms, you can specify the AND or the OR Boolean operator simply by clicking a button (see Lesson 2, "Searching the Web," for details on Boolean operators). You do not need to enter exact association names in the search engine so you may get pretty good results if you enter a broad subject term. For example, the term **forest products** will retrieve information about the Independent Forest Products Association. The term **marketing** will retrieve information about several organizations, including the American Marketing Association and the Direct Marketing Association.

5. If you use a subject term, you may want to enlarge the number in the scrollbox beside the text that says Maximum # of Associations to Retrieve.

6. After you've typed your terms and adjusted the scrollbox, click the GO! button. Your search results will include the names of organizations matching your search criteria. To visit a site, just click the organization's name.

BROWSING CATEGORIES IN ASSOCIATIONS ON THE NET

The Internet Public Library, described in Lesson 4, "Checking Out Internet Libraries," offers another way to find organizations' Web sites. The IPL's Associations on the Net (AON) is a collection of links to more than 500 sites in these categories:

- Arts, Humanities and Culture
- Business
- Computers and the Internet
- Entertainment and Leisure

- Health and Medical Science
- Industry
- Labor
- Law and Politics
- Science and Technology
- Social Science

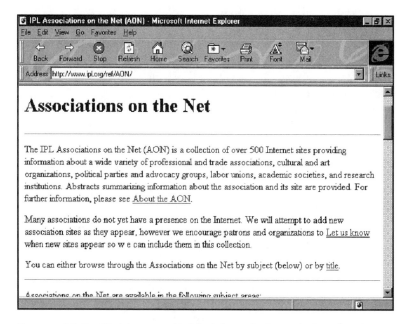

FIGURE 15.2   The Internet Public Library's Associations on the Net lets you browse categorical links to more than 500 organizations.

To browse Associations on the Net, follow these steps:

1. Type the URL **http://www.ipl.org/ref/AON/** in your Web browser's address box and press Enter.

2. Scroll the page until you find a category of interest.

3. Click either the name of a category or a subcategory. (Clicking the category name will give you information on any general references, but few categories have general references.)

4. You will see a list of associations in the category or sub-category you selected. Click the highlighted text near the top of the page that says long version of this page.

5. For each association, you will see a brief description of the Web site. To visit, just click the association name.

Another good place to look for links to associations is the Yahoo! site described in Lesson 2. You can access the Yahoo! business organization category by selecting the Society and Culture category on the home page. Then select Organizations and Business. Or use the URL **http://www.yahoo.com/Society_and_Culture/Organizations/Business/**.

CONTACTING ASSOCIATIONS ONLINE

If you don't find the information you need at an association's Web site, you may want to try requesting data or posing a question to one of the organization's members online. Many associations post e-mail addresses of their officers or even an address for general information requests.

Of course, some people and some organizations are more responsive than others. And some organizations monitor their e-mail better than others. But it doesn't hurt to ask.

In this lesson, you learned how to find and use Web sites sponsored by trade associations. In the next lesson, you'll learn how to find details on trade shows and conferences.

Tracking Trade Shows and Conferences

In this lesson, you'll learn how to find information on trade shows and conferences.

Finding Events with Trade Show Central

The last lesson noted that Web sites sponsored by associations can be good sources of information on conferences, but if you need just conference details and not the other material available from association sites, there's a more efficient way to find the information you need: a trade show database.

One of the largest is available at Trade Show Central, a Web site with a directory of information on more than 30,000 shows worldwide.

To search Trade Show Central's database, follow these steps:

1. Type the URL **http://www.tscentral.com/** in your Web browser's address box and press Enter.

2. On the Trade Show Central home page, click the Trade Show Directory icon (see Figure 16.1).

3. On the next page, you'll see the Trade Show Central Search Utility. It helps you find shows by name, industry category, date, city, or country.

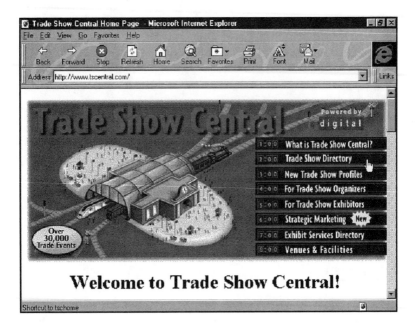

Figure 16.1   Trade Show Central provides a directory with information on more than 30,000 shows.

4. The Search Utility also lets you specify how you want your results sorted: by event name, city, country, or date.

5. After you make your selections, click the Do Search button near the bottom of the page.

6. You'll receive a table showing the location and date of the shows matching your search criteria. For additional details on a particular show, click its name.

7. If you want more information than Trade Show Central provides, click the text at the top of the page that says **Request more information on this show.**

8. You'll receive an electronic form. Fill it in and click the Send Request button near the bottom of the page. Your request will be forwarded to the trade show organizer who will send you additional details.

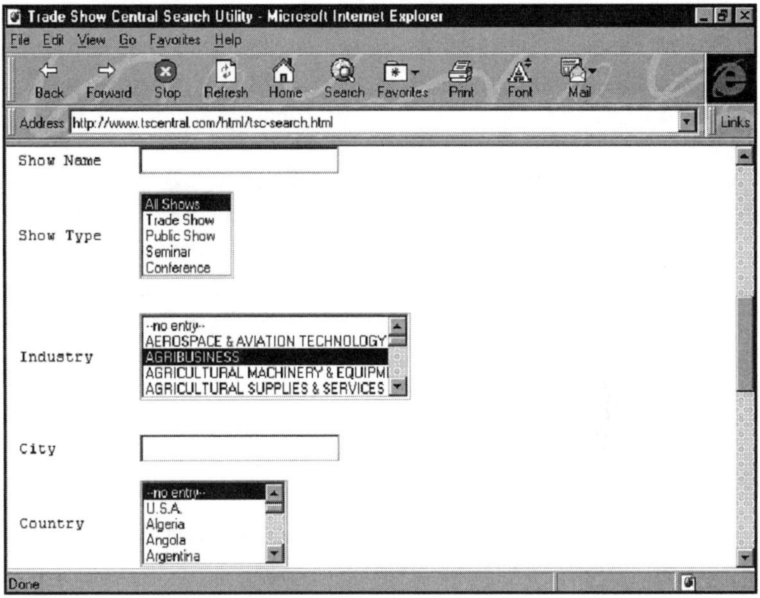

FIGURE 16.2   The Trade Show Central Search Utility lets you use scrollboxes to find specific types of shows.

Trade Show Central offers several other features you may find useful. Look for these menu items on the site's home page (see Figure 16.1):

- **New Trade Show Profiles**—Detailed information on the latest entries in the database.

- **For Trade Show Organizers**—Information about putting your show in the database and letting Trade Show Central design a Web page for your event.

- **For Trade Show Exhibitors**—Information on advertising with Trade Show Central.

- **Strategic Marketing**—Links to companies that provide trade show marketing and survey services.

- **Exhibit Services Directory**—A database of information on more than 5,000 exhibit service vendors.

- **Venues & Facilities**—A database of information on more than 2,000 facilities worldwide, including arenas, amphitheaters, auditoriums, convention centers, hotels, theaters, and stadiums.

FINDING SHOWS WITH EXPOGUIDE

Another Web site with a trade show database is EXPOguide. It contains information on more than 6,000 shows, conferences, and exhibitions. The site also offers several features that may be useful for meeting planners.

To search the EXPOguide database, follow these steps:

1. Type the URL **http://www.expoguide.com/** in your Web browser's address box and press Enter.

2. On the EXPOguide home page, click the Trade Shows, Conferences, and Exhibitions icon (see Figure 16.3).

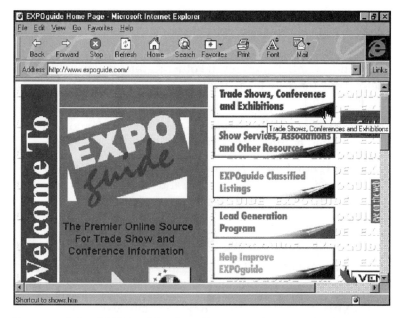

FIGURE 16.3   EXPOguide also offers a trade show database.

3. On the next page, you'll see icons labeled Alphabetical Search, Search by Date, Search by Location, and General Search. For this lesson, click General Search.

4. The General Search engine lets you specify whether you want to search for exact words or concepts associated with your keywords.

> **TIP** **Searching by Conference Name** If you know the name of the show you're seeking, use EXPOguide's General Search option and select an exact search. It's usually quicker than scrolling through lists of shows in the Alphabetical Search.

5. After you enter your keywords and select either an exact or a concept search, click the Search button.

6. You'll receive a list of events ranked from Highly Relevant to Possibly Relevant. To find details about a conference, click its name.

7. If you find a show you like, but you want to see a list of other, similar shows, use the Back button on your Web browser to return to the main search results list.

8. Click the Q in the same line as the show's name. You'll receive a new set of search results with a list of shows similar to the one you liked.

9. When you click a show's name, you'll see basic information such as date and location. For a few shows you can find additional details, including contact information, Web site address, projected attendees, exhibitors, and conference fees.

10. The search results page also has a button labeled Send Me More Information. When you click it, you can fill out an online form that EXPOguide will forward to the conference organizers.

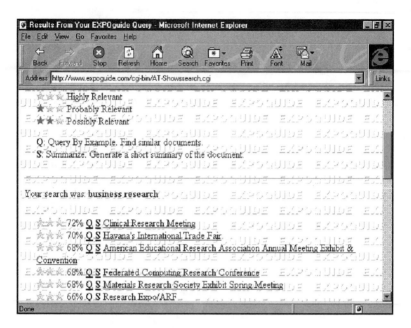

FIGURE 16.4   EXPOguide provides ranked search results.

OTHER SOURCES OF TRADE SHOW INFORMATION

- **TechWeb (http://www.techweb.com/calendar/)** offers the TechCalendar. It can help you find information on conferences worldwide that focus on computers, communications, software, and the Internet.

- **European Trade Shows and Exhibitions (http://www.ring.net/~perfec/euroexpo.html)** provides links to European events.

- **ExpoWeb (http://www.expoweb.com/)** helps you locate conventions, exhibitions, and trade fairs in the medical, computer, telecommunications, gaming, and food service industries.

- **WorldNet Productions (http://www.worldnet.se/)** offers international trade show information. You can search by country, industry, or keyword.

- **Blenheim Group PLC (http://www.blenheim .com/)**, a trade show management company, offers a trade show database called Worldwide Search. A related site, **ShowNet (http://www.shownet.com/)** lists several computer and information technology conferences in the U.S.

News release databases also are good sources of information on trade shows and conferences (see Lesson 8, "Finding Company and Industry Information in News Releases").

If you're looking for information on companies involved in the trade show industry, Yahoo! can help. Go to the Web site **http:// www.yahoo.com/** and scroll down through the following categories: Business and Economy, Companies, Conventions and Trade Shows.

In this lesson, you learned how to find information on trade shows and conferences. In the next lesson, you'll learn how to book business travel online.

17 LESSON

BOOKING BUSINESS TRAVEL

In this lesson, you'll learn how to use the Internet to make travel reservations.

EXPEDITIONS WITH EXPEDIA

If you found a trade show you want to attend at one of the Web sites explained in the last lesson, you may need to make travel arrangements. You can do that on the Web too.

Several sites let you make flight, rental car, and hotel reservations. One of the best is Microsoft's Expedia. After you register (it's free), you can use Expedia's Travel Agent system to search a massive database of travel information. It's a Web version of the same system many travel agencies use.

When you find a flight, car, or room for your trip, you can use your credit card to reserve it online. You also can create detailed itineraries.

This lesson shows you how to create a complete itinerary with flight, car, and hotel bookings, so it involves a lot of steps. But most of them take only a second or two. Plus, you'll be able to book travel arrangements more quickly after you've gone through the process once. Please note that you will not need to make actual reservations during this lesson.

1. Type the URL **http://expedia.msn.com/** in your Web browser's address box and press Enter.

2. On Expedia's home page, click the text Expedia Travel Agent (see Figure 17.1).

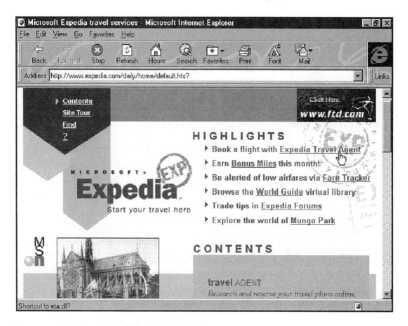

FIGURE 17.1 Expedia's Travel Agent is a powerful but easy-to-use online reservation system.

3. On the next page, click Registration.

4. On the Registration Options page, click the box to set up a free Expedia account and password. If you're a member of the Microsoft Network, click the box that lets you use your MSN Member ID and password. If your browser supports a secure connection, click the box under Security Register. When you've completed the page, click the Continue button at the bottom.

5. You then go to the Customer Information Page. Fill it out and click Continue.

6. On the Confirm Customer Information Page, check the information you entered, read the Expedia Membership Agreement, and click the I ACCEPT button.

7. On the Travel Agent main page, click Shop for Flights, Cars, and Hotels.

8. You may receive a message that says **Secure Sign-In Complete**. Click the text that says Click here to continue.

9. Click Start a new Itinerary.

10. Scroll down the New Itinerary page and click the Flight Wizard icon.

11. On the first Flight Wizard page, select the type of trip you're seeking. Also select the ticket class and number of passengers by clicking the appropriate boxes. For this lesson, feel free to make up the details of a hypothetical trip. Then click the Continue bar near the bottom of the page.

12. The next page lets you type the name of your departure city, airport name, or airport code in the From box. Then type your destination city or airport in the To box. (If the information you enter isn't specific enough, Travel Agent will present another page that helps you choose a particular airport.) You also can enter your departing and arriving dates and times. Enter the date in the MM/DD/YY format. Click the View Calendar bar if you want to choose a date from an online calendar. Click Continue when you finish.

13. The Search Options page lets you choose the airline and type of flights you want. Click the appropriate boxes and then Continue.

14. Your search results will include all the flights that meet your criteria. To see details on a specific flight, click the underlined price next to the flight (see Figure 17.2). Use the Back button on your browser if you want to return to the main list.

US $411.00	5/5/97	5h 51m	New York (LGA) Depart 12:15 pm	to	Chicago (ORD) Arrive 5:06 pm	USAi connect in
(Total: USd 11.00)	5/9/97	3h 13m	Chicago (ORD) Depart 12:45 pm	to	New York (LGA) Arrive 4:58 pm	USAi connect in
US $666.00	5/5/97	3h 46m	New York (LGA) Depart 2:20 pm	to	Chicago (ORD) Arrive 5:06 pm	USAi 1 stopover
(Total: US $666.00)	5/9/97	3h 13m	Chicago (ORD) Depart 12:45 pm	to	New York (LGA) Arrive 4:58 pm	USAi connect in
US $701.00	5/5/97	2h 21m	New York (LGA) Depart 3:00 pm	to	Chicago (ORD) Arrive 4:21 pm	UNIT
(Total: US $701.00)	5/9/97	3h 13m	Chicago (ORD)	to	New York (LGA)	USAi

FIGURE 17.2   Expedia's Travel Agent provides information on all the flights meeting your criteria.

15. When you find a flight you like, scroll to the bottom of the flight detail page. You'll see that you can choose to reserve the flight, add it to your itinerary, or cancel the reservation process. For this lesson, click Add to Itinerary. Also be sure to click the box that indicates you agree with the rules and penalties of the fare (remember: you're not making an actual reservation at this time).

16. Expedia's Travel Agent will display your flight information in your itinerary and let you select from several icons on the left side of the screen. Click the one labeled Car Wizard.

17. On the Search for a Car page, you'll see that Travel Agent has used the information you entered in the Flight Wizard to fill in the boxes for the location and dates you may need the car. Of course, you can override this information

if you wish. On the same page, you can choose the type of car and preferred rental company. Click Continue when you're finished.

18. Your search results will include a listing of rental cars matching your criteria. You can find more details about a specific car by clicking the underlined price (see Figure 17.3).

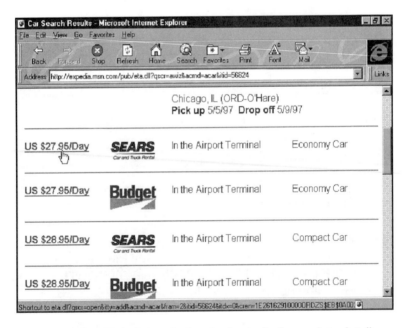

FIGURE 17.3   Click the underlined price to find complete details about a specific car.

19. When you view the details about a car, you can reserve it, add it to your itinerary, or cancel the car reservation process. For this lesson, click Add to Itinerary.

20. Travel Agent will now display your itinerary with both the flight and rental car information. To continue the lesson, select the Hotel Wizard button.

21. On the Location page, you'll see that Travel Agent has used the information you entered previously to determine the city where you want to stay. You also can select a specific hotel or chain. Click Continue when you're ready.

22. The next page lets you choose the prices and amenities you want. You also can choose to search only hotels that can be reserved online. If an online map is available for your city, you can select to have your search results displayed in a list or a map. For this lesson, select the list option and then click Continue.

23. Your screen will look similar to the one shown in Figure 17.4. To see details about a hotel, click its name in the list in the left frame.

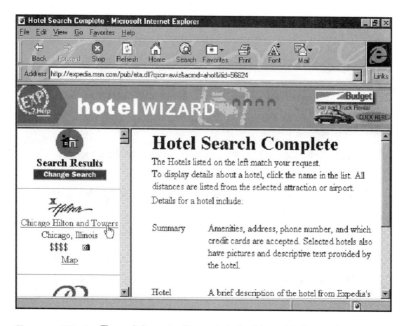

FIGURE 17.4 Travel Agent offers detailed hotel information.

24. Click the bar labeled Check Room Availability.

25. The next page lets you specify the number of guests and the dates you'll be staying. You'll see that Travel Agent has again used the information you provided to fill in the selections. To accept them, click Continue.

26. Your search results will include a list of available rooms meeting your criteria. Click any room price for more details.

27. At the bottom of the Hotel Room Detail page, click Add to Itinerary.

28. Now you will see a complete itinerary. You can edit, delete or print it with the icons on the left side of the page. You can make actual reservations by clicking the bars within the itinerary. Travel Agent automatically saves your itinerary for you under the name of the destination and travel date. You can open it the next time you visit the site by choosing it from a Select Itinerary page. Travel Agent will store up to six unpurchased itineraries.

Besides Travel Agent, Expedia provides several other resources you may find helpful when you're booking business travel. Look for these features on the home page:

- **Fare Tracker**—You can get weekly e-mail listing the best air fares between three pairs of cities you select.

- **Forums**—Message boards let you share travel tips with others.

- **World Guide**—An illustrated guidebook that covers more than 250 destinations.

- **Travel Dispatch**—Stay up-to-date on news for travelers.

- **Weather Watch**—Learn conditions and forecasts worldwide.

- **Currency Converter**—Find instant currency exchange information.

OTHER TRAVEL RESOURCES

The Web hosts many other notable travel sites. Here's a sampling:

- **Biztravel.com (http://www.biztravel.com)** offers an online, interactive business travel magazine; a database of information on hotels, restaurants, weather, and airports; an online reservation system; and a service that enables registered members to track their frequent flyer/stayer miles and points.

- **easySABRE (http://www.easysabre.com)** is the Web version of an online travel reservation service that's been available through commercial services for more than a decade. The Web site lets you choose between the command-driven, text-based easySABRE and a point-and-click graphical version called Travelocity.

- **World Travel Guide (http://www.wtgonline .com/start.html)**, provides an alphabetical index of country information. Entries include country profiles and details on accommodations, inter-country travel, and visa requirements.

- If you want to be able to connect with the online world while you travel the real one, visit the **World Wide Phone Guide (http://www.cris.com/%7EKropla/ phones.htm)**. It offers advice on hooking your modem to phone systems in other countries. You'll also find a table of international phone plugs and links to suppliers of some of the equipment you may need.

In this lesson, you learned how to book business travel online. In the next lesson, you'll learn how to search electronic phone and address directories.

SEARCHING ELECTRONIC YELLOW PAGES

In this lesson, you'll learn how to find phone numbers and addresses in electronic yellow pages.

USING THE BIGBOOK

If you need to look up the phone number of a business in your city, you look in the yellow pages. But what if you want to look up a business outside your area?

You can use electronic yellow pages. BigBook, for example, is a Web site with a digital directory that can help you find addresses and phone numbers for more than sixteen million businesses across the U.S. BigBook also provides special features such as a personal address book, online maps, and a virtual city where you can find real businesses.

To use BigBook, follow these steps:

1. Type the URL **http://www.bigbook.com** in your Web browser's address box and press Enter.

2. On the home page, you'll see a simple search form that lets you enter a business name, category, city, or state (see Figure 18.1). You can type keywords in any or all the boxes.

3. If you aren't sure of the name of the specific category you're looking for, click the word Category. You'll be able to select from a list and then return to the search form.

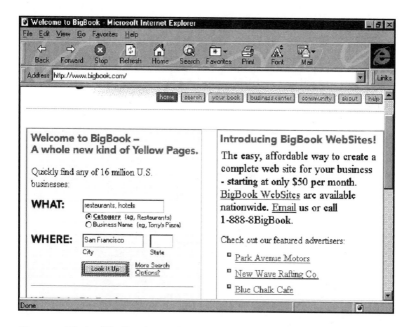

Figure 18.1   BigBook can help you find contact information for more than sixteen million U.S. businesses.

4. If you click the More Search Options button on the main screen, you'll be able to use an advanced interface that lets you search by street address, ZIP code, area code, or an interactive map. After you've entered your selections on either the simple or the advanced interface, click the Look It Up button (unless you're using the map, which lets you click on a location).

> **TIP**
>
> **Searching Multiple Items**   In most of BigBook's search entry boxes, you can enter multiple keywords. For example, you may want to search two or more cities, states, or categories at the same time. Separate multiple items with commas (for example, hotels, taxis, restaurants).

5. Your search results will include the addresses and phone
    numbers of all the businesses meeting your criteria. Click
    the name of a business for more detailed information.

6. Also note the legend or Icon Key at the top and bottom of
    the page (Figure 18.2 shows the legend at the bottom). If
    you see one of those symbols next to a business name,
    you can click the symbol and receive the additional infor-
    mation the symbol denotes.

7. At the bottom of the page, you also can jump to entries
    beginning with a specific letter of the alphabet by clicking
    the letter in the **Jump to:** line.

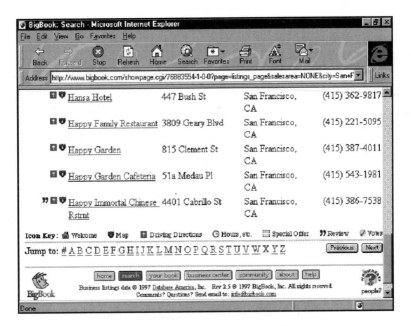

FIGURE 18.2   BigBook offers annotated search results.

BigBook's special features include:

*   **BigBook3D**—Lets you look for real businesses in virtual
    cities.

- **Free Home Page**—BigBook will build a free Web page for your business.

- **Address Book**—Set up your own address book.

- **Maps**—Detailed, street-level maps for more than sixteen million U.S. businesses.

Finding Businesses Worldwide

BigBook is a highly useful resource, but it only contains information on U.S. businesses. What if you need to look up organizations in other countries? Try ComFind, an electronic yellow pages that can help you find companies worldwide.

To use ComFind, follow these steps:

1. Type the URL **http://www.comfind.com/** in your Web browser's address box and press Enter.

2. On ComFind's home page, enter a business category. If you're unsure of the name of the category, you can enter just one word. The next page will let you select from a list of categories containing the word. After you enter the category or word, click the Search button.

3. If necessary, select a business category from the list and click Search again.

4. The next page will let you specify the geographic scope of your search. You can choose to look for businesses in your category worldwide or in a specific country. Note that the Global Search button will list only U.S. companies registered with ComFind. Use the All USA Search to find companies from a complete list of U.S. businesses. To search a specific country other than the U.S., select the country's name from the scrollbox next to the Outside USA Search button (see Figure 18.3). Certain countries may not be listed because ComFind includes only the names of countries with listings in the business category you're researching.

5. If you're searching the U.S. or Canada you can select a particular state, province, or area code. You also can search the U.S. by city or (not shown in Figure 18.3) area code and prefix.

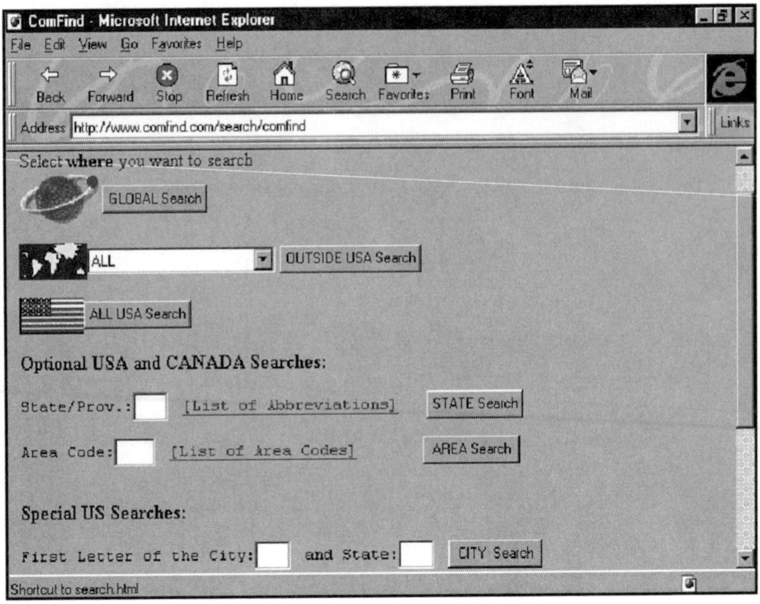

Figure 18.3 ComFind lets you search any or all countries with listings in the business category you're researching.

6. After you make your selection, click the appropriate Search button.

7. Your search results will include a list of businesses that meet your criteria. The first results will be businesses that have provided detailed descriptions to ComFind. These listings are followed by others that have registered with the database. Within the U.S., you can continue your search for the millions of businesses in the database that haven't registered with ComFind. To visit a company's Web page, click the highlighted name in the search

results list. If an online map is available, you can click the
word **Map** that appears in brackets next to the company's
address.

Besides BigBook and ComFind, many other electronic phone directories are available on the Web. For example, both Big Yellow
(**http://s12.bigyellow.com/**) and Zip2 (**http://www
.zip2.com**) contain listings for sixteen million U.S. businesses.

You can find the Web addresses of other electronic yellow pages
at Yahoo! (**http://www.yahoo.com/**) From the home page,
select the following categories and subcategories: Reference,
Phone Numbers, Businesses.

If you want to find Web sites with electronic white pages, which
can help you find the names and addresses of people, choose the
Yahoo! categories Reference, Phone Numbers, Individuals.

You can use electronic directories when you want to contact a
person or company, but there are many other applications for the
information you find. For example, you could search specific business categories in particular areas to create a list of business-to-
business sales prospects. If you need help saving the information
you find with electronic phone directories, see Lesson 6, "Saving
the Information You Find."

In this lesson, you learned how to use electronic phone directories. In the next lesson, you'll learn how to research patents and
trademarks.

LESSON 19

RESEARCHING PATENTS AND TRADEMARKS

In this lesson, you'll learn how to find basic patent and trademark information.

A NOTE ON INTELLECTUAL PROPERTY RESEARCH

Finding patents and trademarks is a highly specialized type of business research—even among professional researchers. You should let the pros handle it if you need comprehensive patent or trademark information you're going to use for legal purposes or for projects that could have significant financial repercussions. Professional intellectual property researchers have the experience and skills to use powerful but complex information systems.

On the other hand, if you need just basic patent or trademark information for general research purposes, you can do it yourself. Patent information can be an especially good source of competitive intelligence because it can help you identify the most significant companies in particular product categories. It also can be an indicator of how much a company is investing in research and development. And it can help you identify the experts in specific fields.

FINDING PATENT INFORMATION AT THE USPTO

The United States Patent and Trademark Office has issued more than 5.5 million patents since 1836. You can find information on patents filed since 1976 at the USPTO Web site. Here's how:

1. Type the URL **http://www.uspto.gov** in your Web browser's address box and press Enter.

2. On the USPTO home page, click the Search Patents button (see Figure 19.1).

FIGURE 19.1 The U.S. Patent and Trademark office lets you research documents filed since 1976.

3. On the next page, click U.S. Patent Bibliographic Database.

4. The next screen lets you choose between a Boolean and an Advanced search engine. They're represented by buttons on the menu bar at the top of the page. You may want to explore the Advanced Search options after you learn the basics, but for this lesson, click the Boolean button.

5. On the Boolean search page, under the Select Database heading, choose either the All button or the Specify button and the years you want to search (see Figure 19.2).

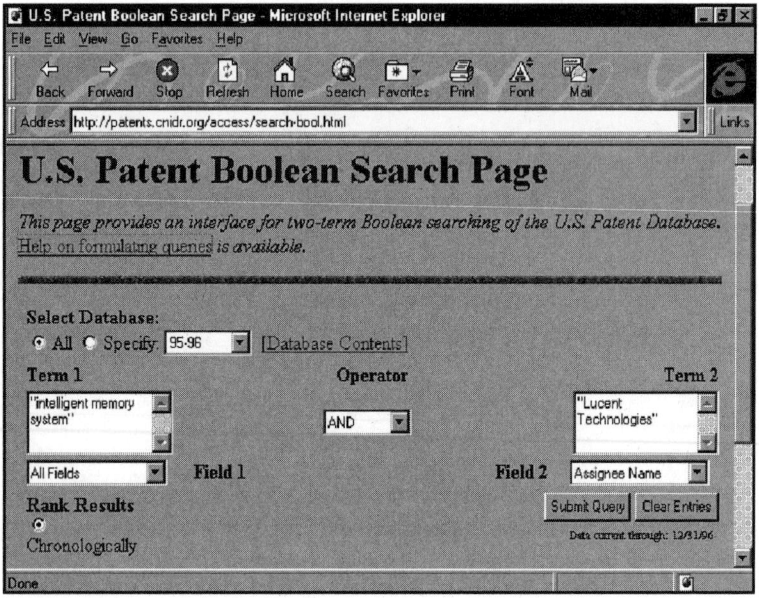

Figure 19.2   The USPTO's Boolean interface offers several search options.

6. Type a keyword in the text entry box labeled Term 1. If you enter a multi-word phrase, enclose it in quotation marks. Figure 19.2 shows that the researcher has entered **"intelligent memory system."**

7. In the scrollbox labeled Field 1, select the part of the patent document in which you want to look for Term 1. For example, if you're doing a general subject search and you've entered subject-oriented keywords in the Term 1 box, select All Fields in the Field 1 box. If you're looking for patents filed by a specific inventor, type his or her name in the Term 1 box and then select Inventor Name

in the Field 1 box. If you're looking for a specific company, type the company name in the term box and then select Assignee Name in the field box.

8. If you want to enter a second keyword, type it in the text entry box labeled Term 2. Remember to use quotation marks for multi-word phrases.

9. Select a field for Term 2 from the Field 2 menu. Figure 19.2 shows that the researcher has entered the field Assignee Name for the company name **"Lucent Technologies."**

10. Select a Boolean operator from the scrollbox labeled Operator between the two Term Boxes. (See Lesson 2, "Searching the Web," for basic information on Boolean operators. If you click the Operator scrollbox, you will see that the USPTO search engine lets you use the relatively rare XOR operator, which was not explained in Lesson 2. XOR means either of your terms can be in the document you're seeking, but not both terms.)

TIP   **Using Wildcard Characters**   PTO's Boolean Search Page also lets you use the wildcard character * to enhance your search results (see Lesson 2 for basic information about wildcards). For example, you could enter "intelligent memory system*" to retrieve documents with either the plural or singular form of the word system.

11. Choose how you want the results ranked by selecting either the Chronologically button or the By Relevance button (not shown in Figure 19.2).

12. Click the Submit Query button. Your search results will include a list of patent titles (see Figure 19.3). To read an abstract, just click the title. If you don't like the results, you can make changes to your strategy in the search entry window and then click the Refine Search button. You also could use the Back button on your browser and start over.

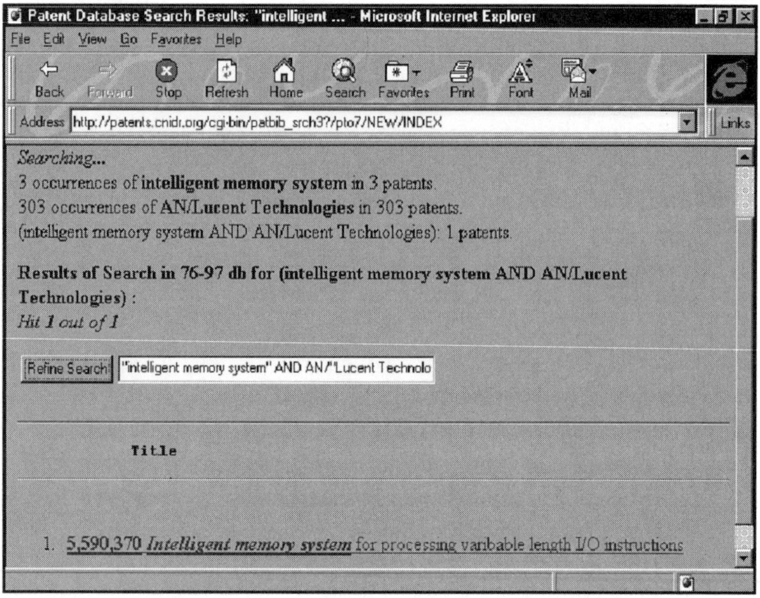

FIGURE 19.3   Click the patent title to read an abstract of the document.

If you want a complete copy of a patent, you can order one from the Patent and Trademark Office. For details, click the Sales button in the menu bar at the top of the page. Be sure to save a copy of the abstract so you can refer to it when you order a full copy (see Lesson 6, "Saving the Information You Find," for information on saving information you find on the Internet.)

OTHER PATENT AND TRADEMARK RESOURCES

Many other patent and trademark databases are available on the Web. Some charge low fees; some are very expensive. Here's a sampling of notable sites:

- **MicroPatent (http://www.micropat.com/)** offers PatentWEB and TrademarkWEB. Various pricing plans are available for both databases.

- **QPAT-US (http://www.qpat.com)** offers a powerful search engine and an extensive database dating from 1974. Designed for researchers who need a patent information often, QPAT-US costs about $200 per month.

- **Chemical Patents Plus (http://casweb.cas.org/ chempatplus/)** offers specialized patent information dating from 1971. Registration, searching, titles, and abstracts are free. There is a fee if you want to display the complete text or images from patents.

- **Derwent (http://www.derwent.com/)** offers patent information in print, online, and on CD-ROM (including several industry-specific CD-ROMs). You can find more information at the company's Web site, but direct access isn't available through the Internet.

- **Thomson & Thomson (http://www.thomson-thomson.com)** offers various trademark and copyright services, including custom trademark research.

In this lesson, you learned how to find basic patent and trademark information. In the next lesson, you'll learn how to find and use small business information.

20

USING SMALL BUSINESS INFORMATION

In this lesson, you'll learn how to find and use resources for small businesses.

ONLINE HELP FROM THE SBA

The Web site sponsored by the U.S. Small Business Administration (**http://www.sbaonline.sba.gov**) offers online resources that can help you start, finance, or expand a small business. Look for the following icons on the home page (see Figure 20.1):

- **Starting a Business**—Provides an overview of SBA programs designed to help get a business off the ground. For example, you'll find answers to the thirty-one most asked business questions as well as details on the Service Corps of Retired Executive, the Small Business Development Centers, and an electronic version of the Developing Your Business Plan Workshop.

- **Financing a Business**—Offers information on the SBA's loan and venture capital programs for businesses unable to get financing through normal lending channels. You can find details on the 7(a) Loan Guaranty Program, the agency's primary lending program, as well as other types of financing that may be available to you.

- **Expanding a Business**—Provides information on numerous resources for growing a small business, including the SBA's export programs, federal government procurement assistance and grants, and the Small Business Technology Transfer Program.

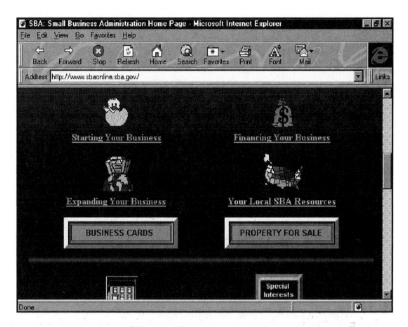

FIGURE 20.1   The Web site sponsored by the U.S. Small Business Administration can help you start, finance, or expand a business.

At the bottom of the main pages for starting, financing, and expanding a business, you'll find links to relevant shareware, freeware, and public-domain software programs. You also can browse or search the complete software collection, which includes more than 530 programs. Here's how:

1. Type the URL **http://www.sbaonline.sba.gov** in your Web browser's address box and press Enter.

2. Scroll down the home page and click the Library of Business Shareware icon.

3. On the next page, you'll see that you can access the collection through a Table of Contents, an Entire List, a keyword Search engine (which allows Boolean searches and wildcard characters), and a collection designed especially for Macintosh computers. For this lesson, click the Table of Contents button.

4. Use the scrollbox to select from such categories as Starting Your Business, Marketing Your Business, and Running Your Business. After you make your selection, click the Submit button.

5. You'll receive a list of available programs. To download and save a program, just click the highlighted text.

Here are notes on some of the other features available through the SBA site. Look for the icons on the home page:

- **ACE-Net**—The Angel Capital Electronic Network connects small businesses looking for investors and investors looking for promising opportunities.

- **Your Local SBA Resources**—An interactive map that can help you find offices in your area.

- **Business Cards**—A place to post your own electronic business card or search for information about other small businesses in specific locations.

- **Property for Sale**—Available property acquired by the SBA in administering its loan program. The property includes real estate, machinery, equipment, furniture, fixtures, and inventory from various types of businesses.

- **SBA Offices and Partners**—Information on SBA's divisions, including the Office of Minority Enterprise Development and the Office of Women's Business Ownership.

- **Special Interests**—Including information on disaster assistance, regulations, appeals, an SBA FAQ, and news releases.

- **Great Business Hot-Links!**—An outstanding collection of links to small business resources; divided into such categories as Business Planning, Congressional Information, Electronic, Commerce, Legal and Regulatory Resources, Procurement and Contracting, Science and Technology, and Women In Business.

TIP

Searching the SBA Site The Small Business Administration offers a lot of online information, so it also provides a search engine that can help you find specific types of data anywhere on the site. Just click SEARCH SBA WEB PAGES near the bottom of the home page. The search engine lets you use Boolean operators and wildcard characters. Be sure to put multi-word phrases in quotation marks (for example, "loan form").

DOWNLOADING DOCUMENTS FROM ELF

Edward Lowe was the entrepreneur who invented Kitty Litter and "brought the American house cat in from the cold—from out of the barn and the alleyways—and turned it into the most popular pet in the U.S."

The Edward Lowe Foundation (ELF) is an organization dedicated to championing "the entrepreneurial spirit by providing information, research, and education experiences which support small business people and the free enterprise system."

The Edward Lowe Foundation's smallbizNet (**http://www .lowe.org**) is a Web site offering numerous resources, including databases and a document delivery service.

The heart of smallbizNet is the Edward Lowe Digital Library, a collection of more than 4,000 book chapters, articles, and other documents from diverse sources, including government agencies, publishers of small business material, universities, and non-profit organizations.

According to ELF, "the documents and book chapters in the ELDL are intended to assist in the start-up and ongoing management of a business." The foundation also notes that "coverage ranges from Advertising to Zoning, and almost anything in between."

To use the digital library, follow these steps:

1. Type the URL **http://www.lowe.org/** in your Web browser's address box and press Enter.

2. On the home page, click the Information button (see Figure 20.2).

3. On the next page, click the smallbizNet Resources square.

4. You'll see a list of ELF's searchable and browsable databases. Click Edward Lowe Digital Library.

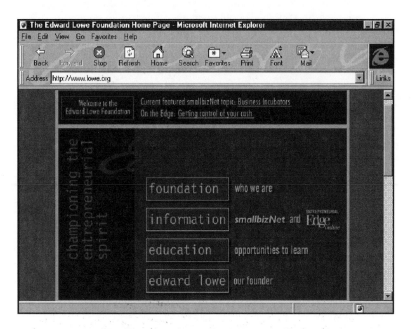

FIGURE 20.2 The Edward Lowe Foundation offers a library of small business information.

5. On the next page, if you want to browse the collection by topic, click the text that says **Topical coverage**. (You also can browse Using Document Categories (Coarse Search) or Using Subject Areas (Fine Search). Just click on the relevant text near the bottom of the page. Using Subject Areas gives you the most detailed information.)

6. To search the collection, enter your keywords in the search entry box. If you click the text that says Tips for Power Searches, you'll see you need to use quotation marks around phrases, and you'll learn how to use

proximity operators for the ELF search engine. You'll also learn that you can use greater than (for example, >1995), less than (<1995), or equal to (=1995) with dates and other numerical expressions.

7. When you're ready, click the Run Query button.

8. Your search results will include document titles matching your criteria. Many of them probably will be free, and you can view them directly on the Web by clicking their titles. Some documents come from commercial publishers and require a royalty fee. Those documents are indicated by a "$" (see Figure 20.3). If you click a document for which there's a fee, you'll see a page that lists the charge (usually $2.00 to $5.00) and offers a link to information on setting up an account.

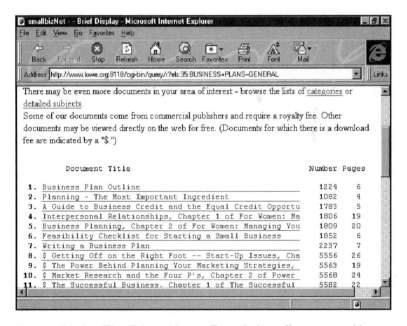

FIGURE 20.3   The Edward Lowe Foundation offers no- and low-cost information.

ELF offers many other resources that could be valuable to small businesses, including a section of books from Oasis Press/PSI Research, Inc., ProSystems Consulting, Self-Counsel Press, and NTC Business books. You can order complete titles by phone, mail, or fax. Prices vary (most are in the $20 to $40 range).

ELF also provides a link to Entrepreneurial Edge Online (**http://www.edgeonline.com/**). It offers a digital version of the magazine, archives of past issues, and interactive forums.

OTHER SMALL BUSINESS RESOURCES

- The **Small Business Advancement National Center (http://www.sbaer.uca.edu)** is maintained by the University of Central Arkansas. The Web site provides the results of small business studies as well as bulletins, publications, databases, and news from organizations such as the Small Business Institute and the International Council for Small Business.

- The **Cyberpreneur's Guide to the Internet (http://asa.ugl.lib.umich.edu/chdocs/cyberpreneur/Cyber.html)** is a list of Internet resources created as part of a class at the School of Information and Library Studies at the University of Michigan.

- **Entrepreneurs on the Web (http://www.eotw.com/)** offers links to various resources, including online magazines and entrepreneurial organizations.

- **U.S. Business Advisor (http://www.business.gov)**, maintained by the U.S. government, is designed to "provide business with one-stop access to federal government information, services, and transactions." Topics include doing business with the government, international trade, finance, labor, and regulations.

- **/smallbiz (http://www.microsoft.com/smallbiz/)**, an electronic magazine from Microsoft, offers features designed to help you start, run, and grow a business. You also can find a guide to entrepreneurial events, information on small businesses around the world, and, of course, details on Microsoft products.

SOHO (SMALL OFFICE/HOME OFFICE) RESOURCES

- The **Home Business Information Center (http://www.homebusiness.com)** is a Web site from the American Home Business Association. You can explore the benefits of membership online. You also can visit a small business forum and sign up for a free Home Business Newsletter, delivered weekly by e-mail.

- **Your Home Office (http://www.smalloffice.com)** is sponsored by the editors of Small Business Computing and Home Office Computing magazines. The Web site offers small business news and advice. You also can find several archived columns.

- **SOHO Central (http://www.hoaa.com)** is the online home of the Home Office Association of America. SOHO Central describes the benefits of membership, offers "50 Great Home Office Start-up Ideas," and provides links to other home office sites.

In this lesson, you learned how to find small business resources. In the next lesson, you'll learn how to use online tax and accounting information.

USING TAX AND ACCOUNTING RESOURCES

In this lesson, you'll learn how to find and use Web sites offering tax and accounting information.

ONLINE WITH THE IRS

Perhaps the IRS is trying to put on a friendly face. When you first connect with the agency's Web site, you'll see The Digital Daily. It's designed to look like a tabloid newspaper—complete with silly headlines and photos—and it may make you doubt that you can find useful information.

But you can find many helpful resources at the site. In fact, the IRS has done an exemplary job of creating a Web site with a large collection of useful information and online services. For example, you can download nearly 700 official forms, instructions, and publications. Here's how:

1. Type the URL **http://www.irs.ustreas.gov/prod/ cover.html** in your Web browser's address box and press Enter.

2. Scroll to the bottom of the home page and click Forms & Pubs.

3. On the next page, you'll see links to several areas. The first two let you browse IRS documents. Just click either Publications or Forms And Instructions.

4. Whether you're using the Publications or Forms And Instructions page, click the button that indicates the format

in which you would like to download documents. You probably will want to select the PDF format, which was explained in Lesson 6, "Saving the Information You Find." For information on the other formats, click the acronyms (see Figure 21.2).

Figure 21.1   The IRS publishes a mock tabloid on the Web.

5. Scroll down the list of documents. When you see one you want to download, click the name. If you want more than one document, hold down the control button while you click another name.

6. After you make your selections, go to the bottom of the page and click the Download Selected Files button.

7. A page will appear with links to the document or documents you requested. Click a document's title to download and save it to your computer.

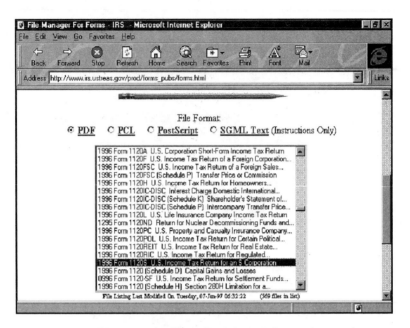

FIGURE 21.2   You can download nearly 700 forms, instructions, and publications from the IRS site.

If you want to search for documents instead of scrolling through the list, click Search For A File on the main Forms & Pubs page. Then you'll be able to use a simple keyword search engine (see Figure 21.3).

> **TIP**   **Use Keyword Variations**   If you don't find the forms you need when you use the IRS search engine, try variations on your keywords. For example, if you use the keywords "home office," you won't find any documents, but if you enter "business use of home," your search results will include Publication 587 "Business Use of Your Home" and Form 8829 "Expenses for Business Use of Your Home."

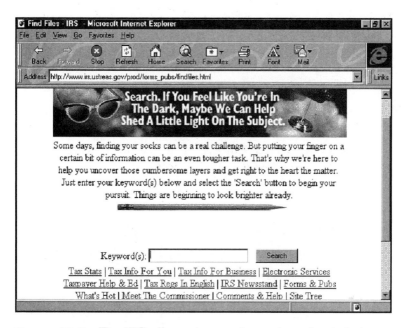

FIGURE 21.3   The IRS offers a keyword search engine to help you find specific documents.

The IRS also offers a section called Tax Info For Business. To access it, just look for and click those words on the bottom of the home page (and most of the other pages) at the IRS site. Information available through the Tax Info For Business section includes the following:

- **Publication 334**—Contains complete directions for business tax filing. You'll find sample tax returns and associated forms, tables, and worksheets.

- **Independent Contractor or Employee?**—Publication 1976 explains the difference. It's available here in the PDF format. You also can access IRS training materials on worker classification.

- **Internal Revenue Bulletins**—Including Treasury Decisions, Executive Orders, Tax Conventions, Legislation, and Court Decisions.

- **Help For Small Business**—Details on IRS programs and services for small businesses.

- **Tax Tips Newsletter, Publication 1558**—A monthly publication for new business owners.

- **Your Business Tax Kit**—A packet of federal forms and publications for employers.

- **U.S. Business Advisor**—A link to the site designed as a one-stop resource for all the services and information the U.S. government offers to business.

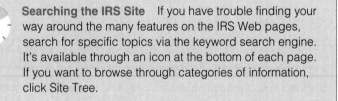

TIP   **Searching the IRS Site**   If you have trouble finding your way around the many features on the IRS Web pages, search for specific topics via the keyword search engine. It's available through an icon at the bottom of each page. If you want to browse through categories of information, click Site Tree.

FINDING STATE TAX INFORMATION

To help you find state tax information, the IRS site offers a link to the site maintained by the Federation of Tax Administrators (**http://sso.org/fta/link.html**), which, in turn, offers links to state sites.

Another useful guide to state tax information can be found at a directory called Cites, Sites, and More Sights. Created by CPA Barry Rubin, the directory includes a Links to States section. It provides access to the Web sites (if they exist) of each state, the agency responsible for collecting its taxes, and state statutes.

To use Links to States, follow these steps:

1. Type the URL **http://home1.gte.net/brcpa/index .htm** in your Web browser's address box and press Enter.

2. Scroll down the page and click Links to States.

3. You'll see a table of links (see Figure 21.4). Click a state name to visit the official state Web site. Click the circles to visit the revenue department and state statute sites. An X indicates that the state hasn't established Web sites in those categories. To download forms in the PDF format, click a document symbol. To connect with a state's faxback service, click a telephone symbol. To connect with a state's FTP site, click the small computer symbol.

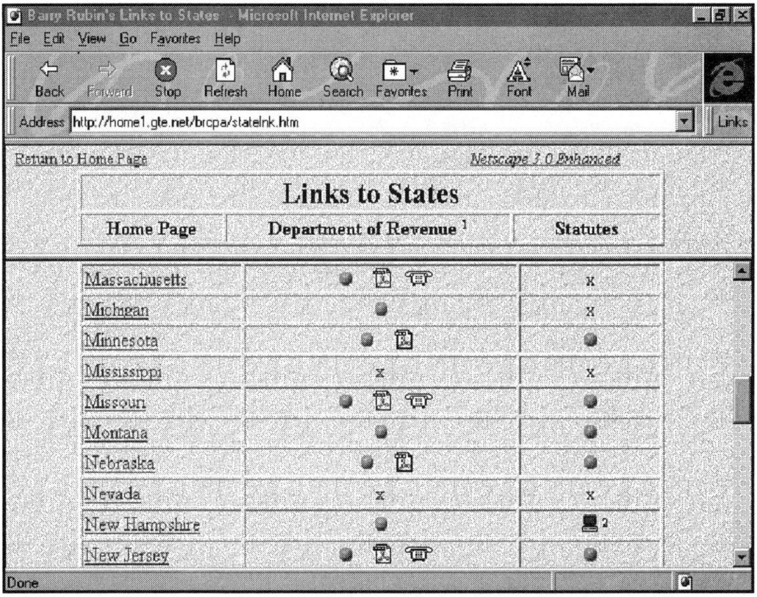

Figure 21.4   The Links to States page can connect you with official state Web sites and tax forms.

Online Accounting Firms

Ernst & Young offers a unique online consulting service called ERNIE. It's not cheap; the cost is $6,000 annually. But you can get answers to unlimited questions from Ernst & Young professionals knowledgeable about the industry, topic, or issue on which you need advice.

After you pose your questions at a private Web site, you'll receive an answer within two business days. You can ask about virtually any business topic, including taxation, accounting, finance, human resources, technology, process improvement, real estate construction, health care, and retail. For more information, visit the site **http://ernie.ey.com/**. The Web address for the home page of Ernst & Young's U.S. office is **http://www.ey.com/**.

Here are the addresses for the other Big Six accounting firms:

- **Arthur Andersen & Co.—http://www.arthurandersen.com/**

- **Coopers & Lybrand L.L.P.—http://www.colybrand.com/**

- **Deloitte & Touche Online—http://www.dttus.com** (Deloitte & Touche also offers **DT Online (http://www.dtonline.com/)**, a site with personal finance and small business information.)

- **KPMG International—http://www.kpmg.com/**

- **Price Waterhouse—http://www.pw.com/**

Other Tax and Accounting Resources

- **Tax Related Sites (http://www.abanet.org/tax/sites.html)** is a directory sponsored by the American Bar Association. You'll find links to federal, state, judicial, and foreign tax information.

- **Tax Resources (http://www.biz.uiowa.edu/misc/links/acct_tax.html)**, another directory, covers more than a dozen categories, including Tax Pages of CPA Firms. Tax Resources was created by the College of Business Administration at the University of Iowa.

- The **Site Seeker (http://www.kentis.com/ siteseeker.html)** is "a directory of resources and sites for accounting professionals and financial executives." It's sponsored by Kent Information Services, Inc., publisher of CPA guides to the Internet. Look in the Vendors section for a guide to Accounting and Tax Software Publishers.

- **Tax Sites (http://www.uni.edu/schmidt/tax .html)**, created by an associate professor of accounting at the University of Northern Iowa, is a directory of sites in 20 categories.

- The complete Internal Revenue Code is available online as part of the **U.S. Code site** from the U.S. House of Representatives **(http://law.house.gov/usc.htm)**. Please note: The code is highly complex information.

- You can ask questions and discuss answers in the newsgroups **misc.taxes** and **misc.taxes.moderated**. (See Lesson 14, "Using Newsgroups to Gather Information," for more information about newsgroups.)

Please note: Most of the tax and accounting information you find on the Internet is reliable, but it isn't a substitute for the services of a tax or accounting professional who is familiar with the details of your business or your particular situation.

In this lesson, you learned how to find and use online tax and accounting resources. In the next lesson, you'll learn how to access international trade data.

LESSON 22

FINDING INTERNATIONAL TRADE DATA

In this lesson, you'll learn how to use online sources of international trade information.

USING STAT-USA

Bill Clinton and Newt Gingrich have at least one thing in common: They both want a great deal of government information to be accessible to the public in an electronic format.

The result is that there is enough government data online to fill several libraries. This is good news for business researchers—especially for those interested in international trade.

Under the 1988 Omnibus Trade Act, the U.S. Commerce Department created the Office of Business Analysis, which was charged with collecting international trade data from other government agencies. In 1994 the Office of Business Analysis closed and reopened as STAT-USA, an independent, self-supporting service that offers an extensive collection of government export and trade information, including trade leads, market research reports, directories of companies involved in trade, and details on specific countries. You often can use the site not only to identify new global markets but also to determine the best approaches to those markets.

STAT-USA charges a subscription fee of $150 annually. Quarterly subscriptions are available, too. If you want to try before you buy, you can take a Test Drive. Here's how:

1. Type the URL **http://www.stat-usa.gov** in your Web browser's address box and press Enter.

2. On the home page, click the Test Drive button (see Figure 22.1).

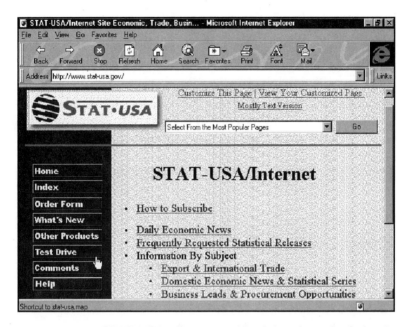

FIGURE 22.1   STAT-USA offers a wealth of data from the federal government.

3. The next page will let you view samples of economic press releases, search economic and trade databases, or read about how STAT-USA information is being used by other companies. For this lesson, click Query a Subset of the Economic and Trade Databases.

4. On the next page, you'll see links that take you to the National Trade Data Bank, the Trade Opportunity Program, or the Commerce Business Daily and the Defense Logistics Agency's Procurements. For this example, click Query the National Trade Data Bank.

5. The next page will present a box where you can enter either keywords (for example, health food markets) or a question in plain English (for example, Where are the best markets for health foods?).

6. After you enter your keywords or question, use the scrollbox to select whether you want to receive the top 50, 100, or 150 documents.

7. Click the Submit Query button.

8. Your search results will include a list of documents containing your keywords or words from your question. To read a document, just click the title (see Figure 22.2).

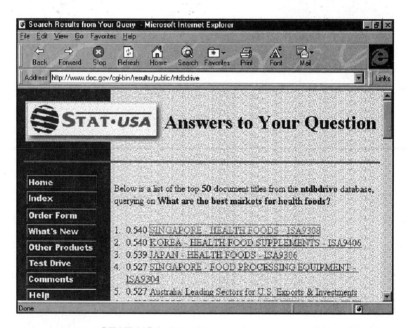

FIGURE 22.2   STAT-USA documents can help you pinpoint trade opportunities.

If you subscribe to STAT-USA you can create your own home page that automatically presents you with the data you're interested in most often. Just click the Customize This Page link at the top of the home page and fill out the brief worksheet. The next time you visit STAT-USA, you can view your personalized interface by clicking the text that says View Your Customized Page.

ACCESSING THE INTERNATIONAL TRADE ADMINISTRATION SITE

Another excellent source of online trade information is the Web site developed by the International Trade Administration (**http://www.ita.doc.gov**). With the motto "...dedicated to helping U.S. businesses compete in the global marketplace...," the ITA offers overviews of international trade markets and advice for succeeding in them.

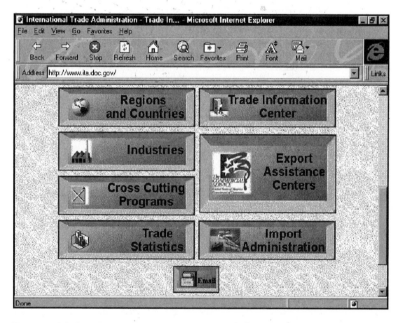

FIGURE 22.3   The International Trade Administration offers several resources designed to help American companies compete in foreign markets. Part of the ITA's home page is shown here.

Features at the ITA site include the following:

- **Regions and Countries**—Information on most of the leading markets of the world.

- **Industries**—Coverage of key industrial and services clusters: Technology and Aerospace, Tourism, Basic Industries, Environmental Technologies, Service Industries and Finance, and Textiles, Apparel, and Consumer Goods.

- **Cross Cutting Programs**—Information on export programs and initiatives such as the Advocacy Center, Big Emerging Markets, FTAA2005, and American Business Centers overseas.

- **Trade Statistics**—International trade data and economic analysis.

- **Trade Information Center**—FAQs and directories of export assistance contacts and programs.

- **Export Assistance Centers**—Information on the centers' services and locations. Export Assistance Centers are designed to help small- and medium-sized U.S. businesses.

- **Import Administration**—Information on antidumping and countervailing duty legislation as well as details on the Foreign Trade Zones program.

OTHER INTERNATIONAL TRADE RESOURCES

- The **Office of the U.S. Trade Representative (http://www.ustr.gov)** provides information such as the National Trade Estimate Report on Foreign Trade Barriers. It's divided into sections focusing on individual countries.

- The **U.S. Department of State (http://www.state.gov)** offers information on countries worldwide. Look in the Business Services and Travel areas of the site.

- The **CIA World Fact Book** (**http://www.odci.gov/ cia/publications/95fact/index.html**) contains detailed political, social, and economic information for countries around the world.

DIRECTORIES

- **Best International Trade Web Sites** (**http:// 199.106.95.11/dolphin/tradelnk.html**) is a guide to government agencies, companies, and international organizations. Rankings and reviews are available for several sites.

- **WorldClass SuperSite** (**http://web.idirect.com/ ~tiger/**) is a guide to more than 600 business sites from seventy countries. The Trade category covers world business directories, ports, cargo handlers, and trade tools such as software, charts, and translation services.

- **Rexco's International Trade Resources** (**http:// www.rexco.com/rexco/index.html**) covers electronic trade, organizations, reference resources, and other trade sites around the world.

In this lesson, you learned how to find and use international trade information. In the next lesson, you'll learn about the business resources available through America Online.

USING BUSINESS RESOURCES ON AMERICA ONLINE

In this lesson, you'll learn how to find and use America Online's business resources.

WHAT BUSINESS INFORMATION DOES AOL OFFER?

America Online is an electronic community, an e-mail system, an Internet gateway, a live chat room host, and an information provider on topics ranging from setting up a Web site to buying a new car to cooking Spanish tapas.

AOL also offers a large collection of high-quality business information. You can find resources that help you track business news, explore electronic commerce, find small business advice, read digital publications, and even set up a private online area for your company.

TRACKING BUSINESS NEWS

To provide business news, AOL collects information from wire services such as Reuters and makes it available through a single, frequently updated news service. To access it, follow these steps:

1. Click the Today's News button on the main channel screen. Or click the Keyword button on the menu bar, type in the Keyword **News**, and click the Go button.

2. The first news screen will show you the top U.S. and international stories. Look for the Business area and click the Highlights button.

3. The screen will change to highlight business news (see Figure 23.1). News summaries will be displayed in the center window. Top Stories, photos, and graphics will appear directly below the summaries. To view a top story, photo, or graphic, double-click the title.

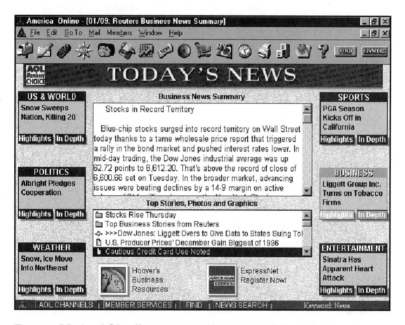

FIGURE 23.1   AOL offers an easy way to track business news.

4. For more news, click the In Depth button under the Business section.

5. You'll see resources you can use to gather detailed Industry News or International Business News. Just click the arrows beside those words.

6. In either the Industry News or International Business News areas, you can search for specific companies or

topics through the News Search button at the bottom of
the screen. Information in news areas is compiled from
Reuters, the Associated Press, Business Wire, and PR
Newswire. Articles are kept online for a minimum of three
days.

> **TIP** **Using News Profiles** AOL's News Profiles service
> tracks the articles you're interested in and delivers them
> to you as e-mail. You then could read the articles offline,
> and you won't miss information because of the three-day
> limit mentioned above. You can set up your profiles by
> selecting keywords that identify the type of information
> you're interested in. For example, if you want to track
> news about Microsoft, you can set up a profile to search
> news and business wires for all the articles containing the
> company's name. The primary sources for the service are
> The Associated Press, PR Newswire and Business Wire.
> You can set up to five profiles per screen name. There is
> no charge for the service. For more information, use the
> keyword **News Profiles.**

There are many other resources available through the In Depth
news screen. If you use the Search Company News by Ticker
feature, you can find information in a fourteen-day archive of
Associated Press and Reuters stories as well as a 30-day archive
of stories from Business Wire and PR Newswire. If you don't know
the ticker symbol for a company, use the Look Up Ticker button
to search through a listing of more than 19,000 publicly-traded
companies.

The New York Times Business News area provides daily headlines
and complete articles from the *Times* business section. You also
can search for stories on specific topics, participate in message
boards, and visit a special Computers and Technology area.

KEEPING UP WITH THE DOW JONES

Another good place to track news on AOL is the Dow Jones Business Center. It provides timely information on companies, industries, the financial markets, the economy, and anything affecting the business environment.

Dow Jones editors select news for the Business Center from such sources as the Dow Jones News Service, *The Wall Street Journal*, and *Barron's*. The editors update selected information on the financial markets every half hour. They update top stories many times throughout the business day.

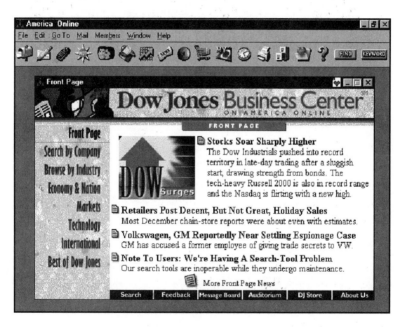

FIGURE 23.2   The Dow Jones Business Center can help you track news on companies, industries, markets, and the economy.

The menu on the left side of most screens in the Business Center gives you instant access to various features.

- **Front Page**—The most important news of the day (see Figure 23.2). You can go to the Front Page from anywhere in America Online with the keywords **Dow Jones**.

- **Search By Company**—Lets you look for news about a specific company. You can search by company name or ticker symbol. Dow Jones stores news for up to 30 days. Go directly to this area with the keywords **DJ Search**.

- **Browse By Industry**—Lets you look through categories for breaking news on nearly 30 industries. Keywords: **DJ Browse**.

- **Economy & Nation**—Focuses on the economy, politics, and other issues that affect the business world. Keywords: **DJ Economy**.

- **Markets**—Provides coverage of all major markets. Look for frequent updates to key stock indexes and indicators for bond, credit, currency, and commodities markets. Keywords: **DJ Markets**.

- **Technology**—Highlights news about computers, software, telecommunications, and other high-tech topics. Keywords: **DJ Tech**.

- **International**—Focuses on global markets and business news around the world. Keywords: **DJ Intl**.

- **Best of Dow Jones**—Provides selected articles from Dow Jones publications such as the *National Business Employment Weekly*, *Barron's*, and *The Wall Street Journal* (including the Asian and European editions). Covered topics include career development, health, personal finance, small business, travel, and work and family issues. Keywords: **Best of Dow Jones**.

The tool bar at the bottom of many Business Center screens includes a Search button. Use it to look for specific companies or subjects in a 30-day archive of articles.

The Feedback button lets you send e-mail directly to Dow Jones editors. The Message Board is a public forum for sharing thoughts about articles in the Business Center. The Auditorium hosts experts in a subject related to Business Center news. The DJ Store lets you subscribe to Dow Jones publications. The About Us area offers detailed information on Dow Jones and the Business Center.

CREATING SUCCESS WITH YOUR BUSINESS

Your Business is an area of AOL designed especially for entrepreneurs and small business owners. If offers the following features:

- **Industries & Niches**—Conference rooms and message boards focusing on specific types of business (for example, biotechnology, construction, real estate).

- **Regional Resources**—A guide to government business services and a way to meet other entrepreneurs in your area.

- **Business Talk**—Live chats and message boards focusing on miscellaneous business topics.

- **Your Business Store**—Online shopping for office supplies, computer equipment, books, and business services.

The middle of the screen features the Your Business Newstand. It provides small business news from such sources as The SOHO Daily News, Home Office Computing, and Inc. Online.

The right side of the screen provides links to information on various entrepreneurial topics—from ways to start making your business dream come true to tools and reference resources.

The Working the Web section will be of particular interest to people who want to explore doing business in cyberspace. Working the Web offers an overview of the benefits of creating your own Web site, advice and software to help you do it, and information on how to get it online.

FIGURE 23.3   Your Business is a resource designed especially for entrepreneurs and small business owners.

CREATING A PRIVATE ONLINE AREA WITH ENTERPRISE ONLINE

Companies that want to take the idea of doing business in cyberspace a step further may be interested in Enterprise Online. Designed to combine the best features of online services, the Internet, and groupware, Enterprise Online lets companies create private areas on AOL.

Businesses can use those areas for internal applications such as conferencing and searching company databases. The private areas also can help companies connect with suppliers, customers, and other authorized audiences. Enterprise Online supports secure transactions and can be used to create virtual storefronts.

Companies can create the private areas based on America Online's infrastructure, Internet technologies, or both. Each option has advantages and disadvantages in terms of ease of use, functionality, technical support, and cost. For more information and an online demonstration, use the keyword **EOL**.

OTHER BUSINESS RESOURCES ON AOL

- **Company Research (Keywords: Company Research)** offers information on stock reports, financial statements, earnings, estimates, 10Ks, 10Qs, and historical stock quotes. The information is derived from several high-quality sources, including Disclosure, Morningstar, First Call, and Prophet.

- The **Market News Center (MNC)** provides news and charts on financial markets.

- **Hoover's Business Resources (Hoovers)** offers an extensive database of basic company information.

- **Nightly Business Report (NBR)** is an online version of the popular television program.

- **Business Travel Center (Business Travel)** offers links to help you book business travel online. Other features include dining, hotel, and city guides as well as information on frequent traveler programs.

- The **AT&T Toll-Free Internet Directory (800 Directory)** lets you browse by category or search by company name.

- The **U.S. Small Business Administration (SBA)** offers extensive information on how to start, finance, and grow a business.

- **American Business Information (ABI)** offers an electronic yellow pages.

- **Incorporate Now (Incorporate)** provides information on incorporating a business.

- **CCH Business Owners Toolkit (CCH)** provides various resources for small businesses, including model documents, spreadsheet templates, and checklists. You also can visit message and chat rooms, track news, and find advice on everything from starting to leaving a small business.

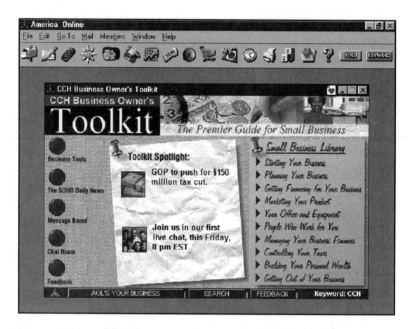

FIGURE 23.4   CCH Business Owners Toolkit offers model business documents, spreadsheet templates, and checklists.

ELECTRONIC BUSINESS PUBLICATIONS

Many of AOL's electronic publications provide searchable archives and extra material not available in the print versions. You also can find message, live chat, and conference areas.

- **Business Week—Keyword: BW**
- **Crain's Chicago Business—Keyword: Crains**
- **Crain's Small Business—Keyword: Crain's Small Biz**
- **Commerce Business Daily—Keyword: CBD**
- **Guerrilla Marketing Online—Keyword: Guerrilla**
- **Home Office Computing—Keyword: HOC**
- **Inc. Online—Keyword: Inc**
- **Investor's Business Daily—Keyword: IBD**
- **Nolo Press Self-Help Law Center—Keyword: Nolo**
- **Worth Online—Keyword: Worth**

In this lesson, you learned about business information on AOL. In the next lesson, you'll learn about hiring professional researchers.

HIRING PROFESSIONAL BUSINESS RESEARCHERS

In this lesson, you'll learn about resources that can help you find information professionals.

TIPS ON SELECTING A PROFESSIONAL

Occasionally you may not have the time or expertise to perform business research yourself. The good news is that many people are now offering online research services.

That's the bad news, too. Because anyone with a modem can claim to be a professional researcher, you need to ensure that the one you hire truly can bring the necessary expertise to your project. Here are several points to keep in mind when you're hiring a professional:

- Ask about the researcher's background. How long has he or she been involved in the profession? How long has he or she been using online services? Ask for references from previous clients.

- Define your project as well as possible. Tell the researcher not only the type of data you're seeking but also how much you need and how much you already have. Note the resources, if any, you've already consulted. Get an estimate for the project before the work begins.

- Find out if the researcher or the firm he or she works for specializes in finding a particular type of information or if they're generalists.

- Decide how much, if any, you need your research results processed, and determine who will do it. Do you need the researcher to deliver only raw data? Do you need the information delivered in a report?

- Ask the researcher about the systems he or she uses? As this book has shown, the Internet can provide a great deal of basic business information, but much of the most valuable data still is available only through proprietary systems. Your researcher should have access to them and the skills to use them.

- Ask how the researcher evaluates data. With so much information available today, evaluation is a critical part of the information professional's job.

FIGURE 24.1   FIND/SVP is a research firm with several years of experience.

A research firm with a great deal of experience, FIND/SVP, is offering a free, Internet-based question-and-answer service called FINDOUT. You can submit a simple reference question through the FIND/SVP Web site and receive and answer within two business days.

The FINDOUT service also provides a library of recommended information covering several categories, from computers to health to finance. The library identifies not only Web sites but also articles, books, videos, associations, periodicals, companies, and other resources. For more information, visit FIND/SVP at **http://www.findsvp.com**.

FINDING AN INFORMATION BROKER

To find other professional researchers, you can use the list of information brokers at Yahoo!. Here's how:

1. Type the URL **http://www.yahoo.com** in your Web browser's address box and press Enter.

2. Select the following categories: Business and Economy, Companies, Information, Information Brokers.

3. You can browse through the listings and visit sites that look interesting by clicking on the company's name.

4. You also can search the listings for specific topics or particular types of research firms. Just enter your keywords in the search entry box (see Figure 24.2).

5. Select the Search only in Information Brokers button.

6. Click the Search button.

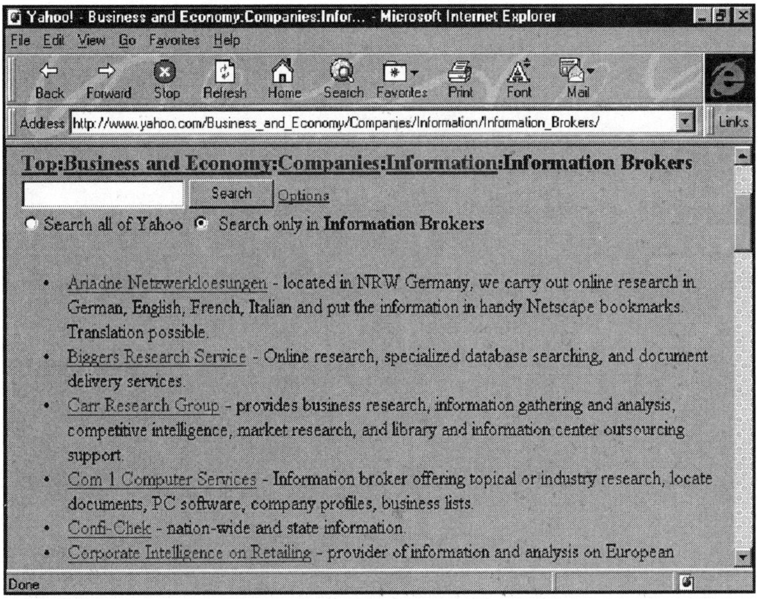

FIGURE 24.2   Yahoo! provides a directory of information brokers.

FINDING A MARKET RESEARCH FIRM

WorldOpinion: The World's Market Research Web Site can help you find a research firm. The site offers a database of contact information on more than 5,000 research organizations in 83 countries. To use the database, follow these steps:

1. Type the URL **http://www2.worldopinion.com/ wo/home/home.qry** in your Web browser's address box and press Enter.

2. On the home page, click Research Resource Directory.

3. To search by name, just type the organization's name in the search entry box and click the Search button.

4. To look for a specific type of research firm or a firm in a particular area, click the Search by Type/Geography tab.

5. You'll see that you can use scrollboxes to select that type
   of firm, country, and U.S. state or Canadian province (see
   Figure 24.3). After you make your selections, click the
   Search button.

6. Your search results will include a list of firm's matching
   your search criteria. Click a firm's name to see contact
   information.

At this writing, WorldOpinion is planning to add new search capabilities to the database. Visit the site for the latest information.

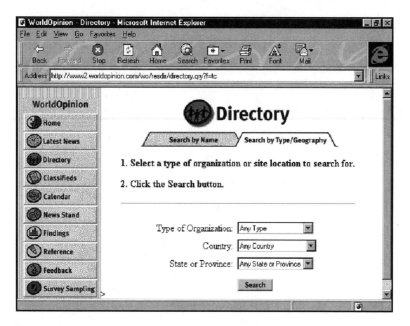

FIGURE 24.3   WorldOpinion offers a directory of more than 5,000
research firms.

> **Don't Forget the Library**   Your local library most likely
> provides a reference desk staffed by information profes-
> sionals who can help you find answers to basic questions.
> For more complex projects, some libraries also offer busi-
> ness research services. You may have to pay a fee, but
> it's usually a bargain.

TIP

INDEX

N

National Fraud Information
    Center Web site, 38
NetPartners Web site, 35-36
Netscape Navigator, 3
New York Times
    (online), 75-76
    archives, 77-78
New York Times
    Web site, 4, 75
news
    business, tracking, America
    Online, 170-172
News Alert (MSNBC), 70
news release databases, 58
    Business Wire, 58, 62-64
    Canada NewsWire, 65
    PR Newswire, 58-61
    PRESSline, 65
Newsbytes News Network, 73
newsgroups, 106-107
    America Online
        participating in, 108-110
        subscribing to, 110-111
    newsreaders, 107-108
    searching content, 113-115
NewsHound, 73
NewsNet, 86
Newspage Direct, 74
Newspapers Online
    Web site, 80
newsreaders, 107-108
    Internet, downloading
        from, 111-113
    Web sites, 112
Newswatcher for Macintosh
    Web site, 112
NOT operator, 16
NYU Stern Java EDGAR
    Interface Web site, 54-56

O

online
    accounting firms, 161-162
    business information
        available, 10-11
online databases
    company profiles,
        accessing, 37-43
        Business Background
        Reports, 37-42
        Hoover's Online, 42-43
        Wall Street Research Net,
        43-44
online newspapers, 75-81
    Atlanta Journal-
        Constitution, 79
    Boston Globe, 79
    Chicago Sun-Times, 79
    Chicago Tribune, 79
    Christian Science
        Monitor, 79
    Detroit News, 79
    Financial Times, 79
    Houston Chronicle, 79
    London Times, 79
    Los Angeles Times, 79
    Miami Herald, 79
    New York Times, 75-76
        archives, 77-78
    Philadelphia Online:
        Inquirer and Daily
        News, 79
    San Francisco Chronicle, 80
    San Jose Mercury News, 80
    St. Louis Post-Dispatch, 79
    USA Today, 80
    Wall Street Journal
        Interactive Edition, 78-79
    Washington Times, 80
online resources
    U.S. Small Business Admin-
        istration, 148-151